KĀKATI GANAPATIDĒVA AND HIS TIMES
(A.D. 1199-1262)

KĀKATI GANAPATIDEVA AND HIS TIMES (A.D. 1199-1262)

Dr. P. Sivunnaidu

KALPAZ PUBLICATIONS
Delhi—110 052

KĀKATI GANAPATIDĒVA AND HIS TIMES
(A.D. 1199-1262)
(Public Interest)

Rs. 360

ISBN: 81-7835-252-4

Published in 2004 in India by
Kalpaz Publications
C-30, Satyawati Nagar
Delhi-110 052
E-mail: Kalpaz@hotmail.com

The book has been published with the financial assistance of
Potti Sreeramulu Telugu University

Laser Typesetting by: Varsha Graphics, Delhi
Printed at: Mehra Offset Press, Delhi

Contents

Preface

This is a study of Kakatīya Ganapatidēva and his times. Ganapatidēva was one of the greatest kings in the history of South India. He ruled over an cxtensive kingdom for a period of sixty three years, i.c., A.D. 1199 to 1262.

Chapter 1—"Antecedents" traces the making of the empire by the precedessors of Ganapatidēva. Ganapatidēva's political life is dealt with at length in Chapter 2—"Ganapatideva on the throne". The next chapter recounts the history of several of his feudatories and officers who stood as strong pillars of the Kākatiya kingdom. The fourth, fifth and sixth chapters sum up the administrative and military organisation and the economic and social conditions during his reign. Appendix—Relations between the Kakatiyas of Warangal and yadavas of Devagiri.

I thank the Librarian and staff of Dr. V.S. Krishna Memorial Library, Andhra University, Waltair, State Archives, Visakhapatnam for permitting me to consult various books and inscriptions in the preparation of this thesis.

I express my sincere thanks to my research director, Prof. Y. Sreerama Murthy, M.A., M.A. (Hons.), Ph.D., Professor of History, Department of History and Archaeology, Andhra University, for guiding me in the preparation of this thesis.

I am indebted to Dr. C. Somasundara Rao, M.A., M.A. (Hons.), Ph.D., Reader, Department of History and Archaeology, Andhra University, for giving me valuable suggestions in the preparation of this thesis. The book has been published with the financial assistance of the Potti Sriramulu Telugu University Lalitakalakshetram, Public gardens, Hyderabad, Andhra Pradesh. I am thankful to the Potti Sriramulu Telugu University, for sanctionship me an amount of Rs. 5,000 as Publication grant.

Dr. P. Sivunnaidu

List of Abbreviations

A.P. Govt. Arch. Series	Andhra Pradesh Government Archaeological Series
A.R.E.	Annual Report on Epigraphy
C.T.I.	Corpus of Inscriptions of Telengana
E.A.	Epigraphia Andhrica
E.I.	Epigraphia Indica
E.H.D.	Early History of the Deccan Vols. edited by G. Yazdani
H.A.S.	Hyderabad Archaeological Series
I.A.P.	Inscriptions of Andhra Pradesh
I.A.	Indian Antiquary
J.A.H.C.	Journal of Andhra History and Culture
J.A.H.R.S.	Journal of the Andhra Historical Research Society
J.I.H.	Journal of Indian History
J.O.R.	Journal of Oriental Research
Ka. San.	Kakatiya Sanchika edited by M. Rama Rao, Rajahmundry, 1935
Kr. Ra.	Kridabhiramamu by Vinukonda Vallabharaya edited by Veturi Prabhakara Sastry, Madras, 1972.
K.A.R.Y.C.	Kakatiya Andhra Rajayuga Charitramu by Chilukuri Veerabhadra Rao, Rajahmundry, 1939.

M.A.S.I.	Memoirs of the Archaeological Survey of India.
N.D.I.	Nellore District Inscriptions in 3 Vols. edited by A. Butter Worth and V. Venugopal Chetty, Madras, 1905.
Nir-utta	Nirvachanottara Ramayanamu by Tikkana.
Sid. Cha.	Siddheswara Charitramu by Kase Sarvappa
S.I.I.	South Indian Inscriptions
Tel. Ins.	Telengana Inscriptions
T.T.D.I.	Tirumala Tirupati Devasthanam Inscriptions.

Sources

An attempt is made in the following pages to give a connected history of King Kākatīya Gaṇapatidēva, who ruled-over an extensive empire from A.D. 1199 to 1262 (63 years). The materials to reconstruct the accounts are few and incomplete. They can be grouped into Inscriptions—stone and copper plate, literature and traditional accounts. All the above categories give information about the life of Gaṇapatidēva. In order of importance the inscriptions stands first. They are contemporaneous and comparatively more genuine. They are inscribed by the orders of the monarch, nobles and private individuals to register grants of land and other gifts to temples, institutions or learned brahmins. Incidentally they give information about the political events, chronology, social set up and the geneology of the donors.

Most of the Kākatīya epigraphs are in Telugu or Sanskrit and very few in Haḍe Kannaḍa. The script used is more frequently Telugu than Dēvanāgari. As against the copper plates which are mobile, the stone inscriptions are earth-fast and can be relied upon to mark the several stages of territorial expansion of the empire. Epigraphs inscribed on stone slabs and pillars, are more numerous than the copper-plate grants in the Kākatīya age. While a long break in the issuance of the records of a ruler could suggest a loss of power, a complete stoppage speaks of his demise. Inscriptions issued by both Gaṇapatidēva and his subjects as well as his neighbouring powers help us in reconstruct the history of this ruler. Literary works also give details about his reign. All the literary sources that throw any light on his reign are either from other courts or of other times, slightly earlier or slightly later. The *Pratāparudrayaśōbhūshaṇaṁ* of Vidyānātha who flourished at the court of Pratāparudra, the *Nirvachanōttara Rāmāyana* of Tikkana, the minister at the court of Nellore and the *Śivayōgasāramu* of Kolani Gaṇapatidēva, form the more important of the literary source material available. They supplement, support or contrast epigraphic information. The *Sakalanīthi sammatamu* of Maḍiki Singana enables us to sketch the administrative pattern of the age, while the *Krīdābhirāmamu* of Vallabhāmatya describes, besides other aspects, the social set up under Pratāparudra.

Chronicles are trustworthy only when supported by other evidences. The *Pratāpacharitra* of Ēkāmranāṭha, the *Siddēśvara charitra* of Kāse Sarvappa, the *Ēkaśilānagara Vrittāṁtaṁ,* the *Kākatīyarājavaṁśāvali,* etc. furnish considerable material about the domestic life, social background of Gaṇapatidēva. Local records provide further information about the contemporary society.

Monumental sources also provide some information for the study of art and architecture of the period. Gaṇapati's fort at Ōrugallu is a surviving specimen of the medieval Hindu forts. His temples at Palampet, Anumamkonda, Ghanpur and other places are the best examples for the study of art and architecture of the period. The friezes on the walls depicting human figures enable us to understand the mode of dressing, pastimes including the styles of natya or dance and aesthetic taste of the society of those days.

1

Antecedents

In the land lying between the Gōdāvari and the Kṛishṇa nestles the hillock, Anumakoṇḍa, giving the sorrounding place the name Anumakoṇḍa vishaya. Here the foundations of the Kākatīya Empire were laid. The story of the builders of the empire goes back to the eighth and ninth centuries of the Christian era.

The origin of the name Kākatīya is steeped in controversy with different writers giving different versions as to its origin. Dr. M. Rama Rao states that the name was derived from the place 'Kākati' the native of the Kākatīyas. He identifies it with the village Kākati which lies near the border of Āndhra with Mysore[1]. According to Ch. Virabhadra Rao, the name derived itself from the family deity[2], or Goddess called by various name as Kākati, Kākatiya or Kākitamma. His arguments are based on the statements in Pratāparudrayaśōbhūshanam and Ratnapaṇam[3], a commentary on *Pratāparudraysobhushaṇaṁ* and Kriḍābhirāmamaṁu[4]. The original *Pratāparudray-śōbhūshaṇaṁ* states that Kākati was their family deity.[5] The *Ratnapāṇam* gives information emplying that the name Kākatīyas was derived from another name of Goddess Durga called Kākati[6]. The Kākatīyas themselves did not categorically state anywhere that they derived their name from their family deity. Nevertheless Mailāṁba, the sister of the Kākati emperor Gaṇapati had clearly stated in her Bayyāraṁ inscription that since the time that king Venna ruled the Kindom from a place (city) called Kākati both he and his descendents came to be known as Kākatīyas[7]. It is possible that the name of the place was derived from the presiding deity which in its turn gave its place was variously identified with the village Kākati in Mysore state by Dr. M. Rama Roa, with Kānker in the Bastar state by Sri C.R. Kṛishṇamachari, with Ēkaśilānagara by Sri Ch. Virabhadra Rao and with the village Kāndahāru in the Nanded district by Sri P. V. P. Sastry[8].

The original caste of Kākatīyas is again a controversial matter and a matter of strong disagreement among scholars[9]. The Kākatīyas themselves are not consistent in mentioning their caste upto Gaṇapati. The Kākatīyas stated that they originated from Chaturthakula and also allied themselves through matrimony with the chiefs of Śūdra caste. But after attainment of imperial status which resulted from the conquests of Gaṇapati they began to claim a Kshatriya origin[10]. Vidyānātha in his book *Pratāparudravaśōbhūshaṇaṁ* does not clearly state the caste of Kākatīyas, he merely says they were superior to those belonging to Sūrya and Chandra lineages[11]. As the Kshatriyas belong to either of these two lineages, it seems to imply a non-Kshatriya origin of the Kākatīyas[12] while those who arrogate Kshatriya status to Kākatīyas exonerate them from that type of concealment. They attribute Kshatriya status to Kākatīyas[13].

Even the origin of the Kākatīyas is steeped in mystery. Till now Bēta I was regarded as the first person or the originator of the dynasty. Though some ancestors of Bēta were cursorily mentioned in the chronicle *Siddhēśwara charitram,*[14] their existence was not established categorically.

Repeated attempts were made to relate one Kākatīya Guṅḍyana of the Māṅgallu grant with Kākatīyas, and on this basis efforts were made to link the Kākatīyas with the Raṣṭrakūṭas[15].

Dānārnava the eastern Chāḷukya ruler issued the Māṅgallu grant in 956 A. D.[16] when his step-brother Amma II fled to Kaliṅga unable to withstand the combined attack of

Dānāraṇava and Kṛishṇa III, the former become the king of Vēṇgi as a result of the support given by the latter.[17] Dānārṇava in his gratitude towards Kākatīya Guṅḍyana who had shown a great deal of heroism in the compaign granted the village of Māṅigallu. The record states the prodeccessors of Kākatīya Guṅḍyana in the following manner.

In the Sāmaṅtavāviṭṭikula was born Guṅḍyana Rāṣṭrakūṭa. His son, a skilled rider, was Eṛiya Rāṣṭrakūṭa. His son was Bētiya, the father of Kākatīya Guṅḍyana[18].

Of the above mentioned persons who sided Dānārṇava, he is the only on termed Kākatīya Guṅḍyana. The suffix Rāṣṭrakūṭa withers away even with his father Beta. There is an etymological connection between the names Kākatya and Kākatīya.[19]

But the resemblence is not by itself an infallible proof of the family relation of Kākatya with Kākatīyas.

The predecessors of Bēta I are mentioned in the Bayyāraṁ epigraph the first Kākatīya record dated in (A.D.1220-1230)[20]. The inscription was issued by Mailāṁba who is the sister of Gaṇapatidēva after the construction of a tank at Bayyāraṁ. A detailed and lengthy geneology from Venna down to Gaṇapati is given, in this inscription.[21]

Venna who was born in the line Dūrjaya ruled from Kākati and from his time onwards his descendants came to be known as Kākatīyas. His son, grandson and great-grandson were all called by the same name Guṅḍa and equalled the three Rāmas, Paraśurāma, Raghurama and Balarama—in valour. Their successor Eṟṟa nṛupati ruled Kuṟṟavāḍi and other lands. He was succeeded by his son Piṅḍi Guṅḍa nṛupati. His son and successor came to be called to Garuḍā Bēta, so called after his anvaya. After killing the warriors Anuma and Koṇḍa, he made their city Anumakoṇḍa his capital.[22]

Sri P.V.P. Sastry identifies the Rāṣṭrakūṭas mentioned in

the Māṅgallu grant, with the Kākatīya rulers of the Bayyāraṁ epigraph on the basis of similarity in the names—Kākartya-Kākatīya, Eṛiya-Eṟṟa, Guṅḍyana-Guṅḍa. He makes the identification in the following manner based on the genealogical charts in the two records.

The Bayyāram grant	*The Māṅgallu grant*
Durjaya	Sāmantavoṭṭikula
|	|
Venna	Gunḍiya Rāṣṭrakūṭa
|	|
Guṅḍa-I	Eṛiya Rāṣṭrakūṭa
|	|
Guṅḍa-II	Bētiya
|	|
Guṅḍa-III	Kākartya Guṅḍyana
|	
Eṟṟa the ruler of Kuṟṟavāḍi	
|	
Piṅḍi Guṅḍa	
|	
Garuḍānka Bēta	

The absence of the name 'Bētiya' in the genealogical chart given in the Bayyāraṁ grant has not failed observation of Sri Sastry but he explained it as premature death of Bētiyas during the life time of his father Eṛiya Rāṣṭrakūta and hence considered important. The forty-first line of the Māṅgullu grant completes the description of Eṛiya Rāṣṭrakūṭa, and commences the account of Bētiya at the end of the same line. But the first three letters are damaged and the forty-second line starts with "To Bētiya nāmadhēyaḥ Samasta Saṁpanilaya stadiyah ..... ". The letters 'abhutsu' were suggested by Sri Sastry to complete the account as 'Abhutsutō Bētiya nāmadhēyaḥ, Samasta Saṁpanniliya stadiyah', who at the same time recognises Bētiya as the son of Eṛiya Rāṣṭrakūṭa. When Bētia was mentioned in the Māṅgallu grant as stated by Sri P. V. P. Sastry, it was due to the fact that he was the father of Kākatīya Guṅḍyana for whose valour Māṅgallu was gifted away.

Inspite of this Sri Sastry hastens to identify Guṅḍyana Rāṣṭrakūṭa with Guṅḍa, Eriya Rāṣṭrakūṭa with Eṛṛa and Kākatīya Guṅḍyana with Piṅḍi Guṅḍa, and completely ignores Bētiya.

If Guṅḍyana Rāṣṭrakūṭa is Guṅḍa III as identified by Sri Sastry the two geneological lists should be identified as follows :

Guṅḍyana Rāṣṭrakūṭa	:	Guṅṭa III
Eṛiya Rāṣṭrakūṭa	:	Eṛṛa
Bētiya	:	Piṅḍi Guṅḍa
Kākatīya Guṅḍyana	:	Garuḍāṅka Bēta
(C. 956 A.D.)	:	(C.1055 A.D.)

If, as maintained by Sri Sastry, Kākatīya Guṅḍayana is Piṅḍi Guṅḍa the identification should be made as follows :

Guṅḍyana Rāṣṭrakūṭa	:	Guṅḍa III
Bētiya	:	Eṛṛa
Kākatīya Guṅḍyana	:	Piṅḍi Guṅḍa
		Garuḍāṅka Bēta

Instead, Sri Sastry conveniently combines the two by making Guṅḍyana Rāṣṭrakūṭa the same as Guṅḍa III and Kākatīya Guṅḍyana as Piṅḍi Guṅḍa. Even this is possible only if Piṅḍi Guṅḍa is mentioned as the grandson of Eṛṛa in the Bayyāraṁ record. This would make the existence of an unimportant father (Bētiya) reasonable. But the Bayyāraṁ record does not mention anything of that type. It only says :

> "Eṛṛa-nāma nṛipatischa tat-parah Kuṛṛavāḍi-mukhasarvva-desapah Piṅḍi Guṅḍa nripatis-tatobhavatkhaṁitārinaranātha maṁḍalaḥ"
>
> (V. 10)

Thus it throws light upon the relationship between Eṛṛa and Piṅḍi Guṅḍa, as that of father and son.

Sri Sastry recognises Eṛṛa and Piṅḍi Guṅḍa as father and son, while drawing the geneology as detailed in the Bayyāraṁ record[23]. But in the geneology he shows Eṛṛa as the grand parent of Piṅḍi Guṅḍa,[24] after the identification of the Māṅgallu and Bayyāraṁ records. The inconsistency is perpertuated when he overlooks Bētiya in the process of identification but thrusts him unceremoniously in his genealogical chart calling him Bēta I (not to be confused with Garuḍānka Bēta or the actual Kākatīya Bēta I). The chart as constructed by him, which identifies the two families, is as follows :

Drujaya

1. Venna
2. Guṅḍa I
3. Guṅḍa II
4. Guṅḍa III (900-912 A.D.)
5. Eṛṛa (912-950 A.D.)
6. Bēta I
7. Piṅḍia Guṅḍa (Guṅḍa III -950-990 A.D.)
8. Garuda Bēta[25] (990-1055 A.D.)

Inspite of P.V.P. Sastry carefully constructing the chronology on the basis of Māṅgallu grant of Kākatīya Guṅḍyana of c. 956 A.D.[26] (identified with Piṅḍi Guṅḍa and called Guṅḍa IV) and Bēta's date of 1052 A.D. (the date of the Chalukya invasion of Chōḷa territory in 1052 A.D.)[27], such a fabrication cannot stand the test as the very identification is mistaken and faulty.

In view of the above mentioned difficulties, the only other possible course to retain and explain the connections between Kākatīyas and Rāṣṭrakūṭas is to reconstruct the whole geneology in the following manner:

Guṅḍyana Rāṣṭrakūṭa	Guṅta III
Eṛiya Rāṣṭrakūṭa	Eṟṟa
Bētiya	Piṅḍi Guṅḍa
Kākatya Guṅḍyana	Garuḍānka Bēta or Bēta I

But here chronology places the greatest hurdle. The Māṅgallu grant gives the date for Kākatya Guṅḍyana as 956 A.D. Because a generation is generally given twenty-five years, his father Bētiya must have been living in 925 A.D. Piṅḍi Guṅḍa, the brother of Bētiya would be his contemporary.

But the son of Piṅḍi Guṅḍa, Bēta I, is known to have participated in the Chāḷukyan expedition of 1052 A.D. against the Chōḷas[28]. The gap between Piṅḍi Guṅḍa and Bēta would be too wide to bridge which makes the reconstruction also impossible.

In view of all these difficulties, the identification of the family of Guṅḍyana Rāṣṭrakūṭa, with that of the Kākatīyas is not possible. Only further research should elucidate the Kākatīya suffix of Guṅḍyana and his relationship with the Kākatīyas.

Yet despite all the inconsistencies and odds discussed above, it is interesting to observe that the Kākatīyas from Eṟṟa onwards came to rule over Kuṟṟavāḍi, which formed the Rāṣṭraka frontier province with their Eastern neighbours, the Cāḷukyas. Whatever may be their affiliations, the Kākatīyas are first recognised as a political force to reckon with in this part of the Telugu country, Kuṟṟavāḍi now known as Koravi.[29] Here they settled down. As time passed of their memories of their origin grew dim and they not only got acclāmatised to their new home but also prepared themselves to laying the foundations of a future Āndhra empire.

It is difficult though, not impossible to reconstruct the chronology of the fore-fathers of Bēta I. Even for Bēta himself only indirect evidence in the form of the Western Chāḷukyan invasion of the Chōḷa land in 1052 A.D. can be asserted as the probable date.

Bēta I, the son and successor of Piṅḍi Guṅḍa[30] was a great warrior who along with his minister and general, Rēcharla Brahma, destroyed the Chōḷa armies and stormed the city of Kānchi[31] though the Chōḷa king Rājādhirāja-I was a powerful monarch who had a great deal of military power at his command. He and his Rēcharla general probably joined the Western Chāḷukya armies that swept into the Chōḷa land in 1052 A.D. during the reign of Chāḷukya Ahavamalla Sōmēśvara-I[32] (in c. 1052 A.D.). The Kākatīyas shifted their allegiance on to the Western Chālukyas of Kalyāṇi, who had supplanted the Rāṣṭrakūṭas (their erstwhile masters).

Bēta by that time killed Anuma and Koṇḍa and occupied the city of Anumakoṇḍa and made it his capital[33]. He ruled upto 1055 A.D.[34] When he was succeeded by his son Prōla II entitled Arigajakēsari. Prōla succeeded in subduing enemy chiefs for his Western Chalukya Sovereign, Sōmēśvara and his son Vikramā ditya-VI. His exploits extended from Chakrakūta, Bhadraṅga purukūta in Bastar, to the Koṇkana Maṇḍala, as the accompanied the young Vikramāditya-VI in his campaigns[34]. As a reward for the services he rendered, he was awarded Anumakoṇḍa vishaya which now became his permanent family fief[36]. With this as the nucleus, the Kākatīya power spread extensively under his successors. Though most of his reign is steeped in battles and wars, Prōla found sufficient time to build the Kēsari or Jagalikēsari tank to irrigate and enrich the lands of his Kingdom[37]. He laid the foundations of a wise economic policy which was perpetuated and emulated by his successors by building a network of tanks and canals providing abundant water supply to lands within their dominions.

Prōla was succeeded by his son Bēta-II by about 1075 A.D. His records appear in 1079 A.D. at Anumakoṅḍa and 1090

A.D. at Kasipet[38]. Early in his career he had the misfortune of incurring the displeasure, which he everted with the help of his Viriyāla and Vēma-Chōḷa allies[39]. It was his minister Vaija-daṇḍadhīsa and Kāma Sāni, the able wife of Viriyāla Eṛra who took Bēta to Kalyāṇi to seek the grace of the emperor Vikramāditya-VI. There, Bēta having prostrated himself at the feet of the emperor, secured the government of the Sabbi-one thousand[40] which probably included the Anumakoṇḍa and the Koravi districts. The infant kingdom thus retained its integrity. To show his gratitude and reaffirm his loyalty to Tribhuvanamalla Vikramāditya, he assumed the latter's titles—Tribhuvanamalla and Vikramāditya[40].

The eldest son of Bēta-II, Durgaṇrupati succeeded him in between 1090 A.D. the last recorded date of Bēta. There is only one record of Tribhuvanamalla Durgaṇrupati dated in 1098 A.D.[42] The next record is that of his brother and successor Prōla-II. It is in 1117 A.D.[43] During a reign of nearly two decades, Durgaṅripati did not or could not achieve anything significant[44].

The tiny Kākatīya principality began to expand under Prōla. He and his neighbours were all feudatories of the Western Chāḷukyas of Kalyāṇi, Any ambition of Prōla to expand would be at the cost of his neighbours and this was possible only when the central authority was either weak or distracted. Vikramāditya-VI was the last of the powerful of the monarchs of the Chāḷukyan line. The imminent downfall of the imperial power did not miss the watchful eyes of Prōla. He fortified himself by a matrimonial alliance with the Natavādi ruler Durga-kshitisa and secured the hand of his sister Muppāṁba. While he merely subdued the Telugu Chōḷas of Kandur, he exterminated others like Govindarāja, Udaya and Jagaddēva and seized the territories of other kings like Guṇḍa's Manthena on the Gōdāvari. His successors stretched their influence over the land lying between Gōdāvari and Kṛishṇa and the modern districts of Nalgonda and Karimnagar. Even Tailapa, the pride of Chālukyas found himself at the mercy of this audacious prince[45].

The brilliant career of Prōla did not last long and he died fighting, after the invasion of Vēngi in 1150 A.D. with a confederacy comprising of the Kōtas of Amarāvati, the Haihayas of Konamaṇḍala and the Malaya Chiefs[46]. Nevertheless, before his death he succeed in exonerating himself from the clutches of imperialism and founded an independent kingdom whose foundations though rugged and ill-laid gave rise to an insignificant and imposing edifice. His chief architect was Rudra-I.

Rudradēva, being the eldest of the five sons of Prōla succeeded him to the throne in 1150 A.D.[47] He was not only a valiant fighter but also an ambitious prince who caused havoc among his neighbours. He was born of Kākatīya-Natavati marriage alliance[48], and had the support of the latter in the wars of expansion. The Anumakoṇḍa or Hanumakoṇḍa inscription of Rudra dated 19th January, 1163 A.D. dwells at length on his various exploits and courageous deeds[49].

Rudra plannned his campaigns in three directions north, south and east and his armies swept the lands of Dōmarāja, Mēdarāja and Maligidēva and the Kākatīya kingdom stretched itself north of Anumakoṇḍa right into the modern districts of Karimnagar to the banks of the Gōdāvari.

Turning south Rudra frightened the Kondur Telugu Chōḷa princes, Bhīma and Chōḍhya and burnt their cities Vardhamāna and Kādur. What happened to Bhīma was not known. He probably perished during the campaigns or subsequently for the Anumakoṇḍa inscription says that those kings like Bhīma, became Gods (i.e., dead) at the very sight of Rudradēva[50].

Chōḍaya made peace with Rudradēva by offering his

daughter Padma in marriage. The Telugu Chōḍas ruled over their kingdom which comprised the modern districts of Nalgonda and Mahaboobnagar[51].

In addition to the Telugu Chōḍa victories of Rudra one Tailapa is mentioned[52], in the Anumakoṇḍa inscription who is variously identified with Tailapa III the Western Chāḷukya king[53] Kumara Tailapa the ruler of Kōduru[54] and with some unidentified neighhour of Bhīma[55].

To the east of the Kākatīya kingdom lies the fertile delta land of the Gōdāvari and the Kṛishṇa, which recognized the over-lordship of the Chāḷukya-Chōḷa Emperor Rājarājā II[56]. Though Kākatīya records found at Dāksharāmaṁ in the Gōdāvari delta, as early as 1158 A.D. Rudra allowed them to be dated in the regnal years of Rājarāja III. In accordance with it in 1158 A.D. Inangala Brahmi Reddy the minsiter of Rudra registered his grant to Lord Bhīmēśwara in the 13th regnal year of Rājarāja II.[57] In only a span of five years from 1158 A.D. Rudra could claim in his Anumakoṇḍa inscription that his empire touched the very sea on the east. In 1163 A.D. his brother Rēpalli Duggarāja made a grant at Dākshārāmaṁ[58], at the end of which the Velanāti cheifs of Vēṇgi, appear in the region[59]. They subjugated the Haihayas of Kōna in 1165 A.D.[60] and the provenance of the records of Velanāṭi Kulōttunga Rājēndra Chōḍa, till 1181 A.D. proves that the Gōdāvari region was under him. This enabled the Kākatīya king to have only a chequered history in the Gōdāvari region. The records of Rudra appear intermitently at Dāksharāmaṁ in 1168[61], 1179[62] and 1186 A.D.[63]

After 1186 A.D. Kākatīyas are not heard of at Dāksharāmaṁ for a considerable period. There were other important poweres like the Velanāti chiefs who had to be tackled first before Rudra could turn his attention to the Gōdāvari delta.

Meanwhile, after the death of Chāḷukya Chōḍa Emperor Rājarāja II in 1172 A.D., his feudatories began to strengthen themselves. Prominent among were the Velanāti Chiefs of Vēṇgi who increased their boundaries on all sides upto Tripurāntakam in the Kurnool district, Darsi in the Nellore district and probablv Simhachalam in the North[64]. They stood between Rudra and his dreams of expansion to the coast.

Around this time an opportunity presented itself quite unexpectedly, by a civil war that brake out among the Palanāḍu chiefs[65], and one of them Nalāgāmarāja invited Rudra to intervene and Rudra instead of supporting Nalagama Rāja effectively subdued his own enemies, the allies of Velanātis, viz., the Kōtas and the Koṇḍapadumati chiefs ruling over Dharanikōta and Nādendla respectively.

When one of the Kōta cheifs Doḍḍabhīma died fighting, Rudra wisely conferred the principality on his son Kēta II and by that strategy gained not only a clear access to power but also the gratitude of Kēta II[66]. Rudra after conquering the Koṇḍapadumatis took no further interest in their affairs but returned to his kingdom in 1185 A.D. His inscription at Tripurantakam dated in that yẹar is considerd by some scholars to refer to the subjugation of the area near Tripurāntakaṁ.[67]

This extension of Kākatīya power into the coastal regions was transient and even the above invasion was facilitated by the death of the powerful Velanāti king, Kulōttunga Rājēndra Choḍa II in 1181 A.D. and the outbreak of civil war among his heirs[68]. Consequently Prithivara was confined to the Gōdāvari delta and established himself there[69]. The remnants of his records indicate that he held his territory till his death. Rudra could not exert himself to bring the land of the Godavari under his rule again as something more interesting occupied his attention.

The two powers Śeunas and Kākatīyaṣ who were formerly the feudatories of imperial Kalyāṇi were destined to build their empires on the dilapidated remnants of that empire and under Bhillma V (1184-1191 A.D.) and his son Jatugi (1191-1210 A.D.)[70] whose imperial clashed there raged a fierce was between the two in consequence of which Rudra was immolated as a victim in the human sacrifice performed by Jattugi[71]. The tragic death of Rudra in 1195-6 A.D. came as a severe blow to the growing Kākatīya power and crippled it completely[72].

As Rudra was heirless, his younger brother Mahādēva (1195-6 to 1198-9 A.D.), ascended the throne, to rule only for a shortwhile. War again broke out between two, and the Kākatīyas once again suffered a reverse, Mahādēva dying on the temple of his war-elephant[73]. His son and heir Ganapatidevā, who had accompanied him, was captured and imprisoned[74]. The Kākatīya glory was completely eclipsed.

As a consequence the Telugu land was plunged in chaos and disorder but the Kākatīya feudatories came to her rescue, particularly one Rēcherla Rudra who stabilised the empire and crushed the rebellions.[75] He then worked for the return of his young master Gaṇapatidēva.

In the meantime Jaitugi realised that to hold down the empire by its annexation is very difficult and prudently set Ganapatideva free[76] after effecting a concilliation. His strategy proved right and peace prevailed for a long time until Yādava Mahādēva himself chose to break up the peace.

References

1. *Ka. San.* p. 8.
2. *K.A.R.Y.C.*, p. 7.
3. *Ratnapānam* by Kumara Swamy Sāmayaji.
4. "Kākitammaku Saidōdu Ēkavira" - *Krīdabhīrāmamu.*
5. "Kākatīyakula Durgadēvi Samaradhanēna". *Pratāparudra vasōbhūshanam.*

6. Ratnapānam by Kumara Swamy Samayaji.
7. *Bayyāram Inscription* (Vol. 8), Ed. by P.V. Parabrahma Sastry in *Bharati*, April, 1967.
8. *E.I.* XVIII No. 41. The Garavapādu grant of Gaṇapati Ed. by Sri C.R. Krishnamachari, *K.A.R.Y.C.*, p. 15; *Bharati*, April, 1967, p. 9.
9. *Ka. San.*, pp. 124-32; pp. 13-15; *K.A.R.Y.C.*, pp. 107-111.
10. *E.I.*, Vol. XII, p. 188; *H.A.* No. 4, I.A., Vol. XXI, p. 197—The Mōtupalli, Pākhala and Kānchivaram Records of Gaṇapati respectively.
11. *Pratāparudravasōbhūshanaṁ*-Nayakaprakaranam, Vol. 13, Naṭaka-prakaranam, Vol. 21, *Ibid.* Part IV, Vol. 4.
12. *K.A.R.Y.C*, p. 449; *J.A.H.R.S.*, Vol. IV; Part 3, 'Some interesting facts about the Kākatiya by Dr. M. Rama Rao; *Kākatiyula charitramu* by Dr. Rama Rao. *Ka. San.*, p. 13 and *Bharati*, April, 1967.
13. *Vidyānāthuni Kākatīyanyaya nirupānam* by Sri Rudraraju, p. 1.
14. *Sid. Cha.*, p. 768.
15. *Ka. San.*, pp. 7-8; *Sid. Cha.* App., p. 26; *Bharati*, April, 1967, p. 7 Dr. M. Rama Rao, in the *Ka. San*, sees a connection between Kākatya and Kākatiya (p. 7), thereby inclining towards a Rāsṭrakūṭa origin, whereas Sri Ch. Virabhadra Rao in his Kākatiyāndhra Rājayuga Charitramu refuses to be convinced by the Rāsṭrakūṭa origin on the basis of the suffix 'Kākatīyas', adopted by Gundyana, pp. 23-28. But Sri P.V.P. Sastry, while editing the Bayyāram grant declares that the Kākatīyas were originally Rāṣṭrakūṭas, by identifying Kākatīya Guṅḍyana and his predecessoṛs, with the Kākatīyas.
16. E.I.XXXI, Ed. by Sri V. Rangachari; Bayyāram Inscription, *op. cit.*
17. The Eastern Chālukyas by Prof. K.A.N. Sastry and Dr. N. Venkataramanayya; *E.H.D.*, Pt. VII, p. 485.
18. *E.I.* XXXI, Ed. by Sri V. Rangacharya. Here V. Rangacharya reads the name of Gunḍyana (II) as Kākatya Gunḍyana, while Ch. Virabhadra Rao, Dr. M. Rama Rao and Sri P.V.P. Sastry reads the name of Gunḍyana (II) as Kākatya Gunḍayana, while Ch. Virabhadra Rao, Dr. M. Rama Rao and Sri P.V.P. Sastry read the name as Kākartya Guṅḍyana.
19. *E.H.D.* Part IX, p. 577.
20. *Ibid.*
21. The Bayyāram Inscription, *op. cit.*

22. The Bayyāram Inscription, vs. 7-21.
23. *Bharati*, April, 1967, p. 4.
24. *Bharati*, April, 1967, p. 6.
25. The names of the successors of Garuḍanka Bēta mentioned in the Bayyāram record are not relevant for the present discussion.
26. *Bharati*, April, 1967, p. 6.
27. *E.H.D.* part IX, p. 578.
28. *Ibid.*
29. Koravi, Manukota Taluk, Telengana.
30. Bayyāram grant—vs. 10-11.
31. *C.T.I.*, Part II, No. 7—Kazipet Ins. of Bēta II, Vol. 1; Bēta I is described as one who earned Goddess Lakshmi by churning the ocean of the army of the Chōla kings. The Palampet inscription of Rēcharla Rudra d. 1213 A.D. in the reign of Gaṇapati, describes his progenitor Rēcharla Brahma, as having flung open the door of Kānchi and promptly brought about the marriage of the Kākati monarch with the Goddess of Victory.

    HAS No. 3. There are different opinions on this Chōla campaign and the identification. Sri Ch. Virabhadra Rao thinks that the Chōla king mentioned in the Kazipet record was not the Chōla king of Tanjore but some petty neighbouring feudatory- *K.A.R.C.*, p. 136. He attributes the victory mentioned in the Palampet record to Prōla I, the son of Bēta I in p. 141. But in p. 142, he concludes that Bēta-I won a victory against the Chōla emperor. N. Venkataramanayya and M.S. Sarma think that it was Bēta-I who defeated the Chōla king of Kānchi.

    E.H.D. Part IX, p. 577 K. Lakshmiranjaṅamu and P.V.P. Sastry hold similar views vide *Sid. Cha.* Introduction p. 34; *Bharati*, April 1967, p. 7. Sri P.V.P. Sastry while editing the recently discovered Sanigara inscription No. 1—d 1053 A.D. different rates Beta's—I victory over the Chōlas from Rēcherla Brahma's storming of Kānchi. He thrusts the latter achievement on Prola-I who does not claim it in his Kazipet inscription of 1090 A.D. *Bharati*, November 1971.
32. *E.H.D.* Part IX, p. 518.
33. The Bayyāram inscription is the first to mention the conquest of Anumakoṇḍa by Beta-I *Bharati*, April 1967.
34. P.V.P Sastry—*Bharati*, 1967, April, p. 7; *E.H.D.* Vol. IX, p. 578. Prōla's

first date is found to be 1053 A.D. *Bharati*, Nov. 1971.

35. Kazipet record, Vol. 3 *Tel. Ins.* Vol. II, No. 1; *E.H.D.*, pt. IX, p. 579.
36. Kazipet record, Vol. 3 *Tel. Ins.* Vol. II, No. 1.
37. *I.A.*, Vol. XXI—Ēkamranātha Temple Ins. Kānchi; *E.I.* Vol. XII, Moṭupalli Ins., p. 188 and Bayyāram Ins. *Bharati*, April 1967.
38. Anumakoṇḍa Ins. *Ka. San.* App. No. 4; C.T.I. Part I No. 6-1079 A.D. December 26; Kazipet Ins. *C.T.I.* Part II, No. 7, d. 1190 A.D. Nov. 24.
39. Gūdur Ins. Warangal district *C.T.I.* Part II, No. 24; *Tel. Ins.* Kākatīyas No. 55; *C.T.I.* Part III, No. 13; Materu Ins. d. 1120 A.D.; *E.H.D.* Part IX, p. 580.
40. *Tel. Ins.* Kākatīyas No.55; *E.I.* IX, 256, Vol. 3.
41. Kazipet Ins., Tel. Ins. No. 1, *Ka. San.* App-No. 1, *C.T.I.* Part II, No. 1.
42. *Ibid.* Recent information extends Beta's date upto 1107 A.D. Jan. 10th, Sangara Ins. No. 2, *Bharati*, Nov. 1971.
43. *E.I.,* Vol. IX, p. 256, Hanumakonds, Padmakshi Temple Ins.
44. Nothing is known about Durgaripathi's achievements or rule. P.V.P. Sastry suggests usurpation by his younger brother Prōla-II on the basis of the newly discovered inscription of Gangaya Sāhini at Kottapalli, Nalgonda District, vide *Bharati*, Nov. 71, p. 11.
45. *J.A.H.R.S.* Vol. XXI, pp.105-6; *C.T.I.*, Part II, No. 3—Hanumakoṇḍa Ins., *E.I.,* Vol. III, Ganapēśvaram Ins. of Ganapati: *H.A.S.*, No. 3, Palampet Ins.; *E.H.D.* Part IX, p. 581-83; *K.A.R.Y.C.* p. 2.
46. *S.I.I.*, Vol. IV, No. 1242; *A.R.* No. 351 of 1893; *E.I.*, Vol. IV, p. 91; *A.R.* Chap. No. 10 of 1916-17; *I.A.*, Vol. XXI, p. 197; *A.R.* 26 of 1890; *I.A.* Vol. XXI, pp. 122, 197.
47. Bayyāram Ins. *Bharati*, April, 1967; *K.A.Y.R.C.*, p. 237; E.H.D., Part IX, p. 585.
48. Bayyāram Ins. d. 1163 A.D., I.A. XI, p. 9.
49. Hanumakoṇda Ins. d. 1163 A.D.- *I.A.* XI, p. 9; C.T.I. Part II, No. 3; *E.H.D.* Part IX, p. 587.
50. *C.T.I.*, Part II, No. 3, Vol. 30.
51. *E.I.*, Vol. III, p. 83; Tel. Ins. Mis. No. 6, Jedesharla, Mahaboobnagar district, Ins. of Kandur Udaya Chola Mahārāja, D. Thesday 25th Dec., 1162 A.D.; *Ibid.* No. 2, Nelakondapalli, Warangal district, Ins. in the reign of Kānduri Udaya Chōda Māharāja d. 1175 A.D. The two inscription reveal that Chodadaya or Kandur Udaya Chōda Mahārāja continued to rule till 1175. A.D. probably after having

made peace with his victory by offering him the hand of his daughter.

52. *C.T.I.*, Part II, No. 3, Vol. 18.
53. "Anumakoṇḍa Sāsnamu" Śēshādri Ramana Kavulu, Sukla Samvatisara, Chaitra, *Bharati.*
54. *K.A.R.Y.C.*, p. 257.
55. *E.H.D.*, Part IX, p. 590.
56. *Ibid.*
57. *S.I.I.*, IV, No. 1107, Dākshārāmam, E.G.Dt.
58. *S.I.I.*, IV, No. 1071.
59. *Ibid*, No. 1086.
60. *Ibid*, No. 1083.
61. *S.I.I.*, Vol. IV, No. 1071.
62. Elliot's collection 15.6.26; p. 207; *Kākatīyula Kalingamu* by Sri M.S. Sarma, *Ka. San.*, p. 178.
63. *S.I.I.*, Vol. IV, No. 1155.
64. *E.H.D.*, Part IX, p. 592-93.
65. *Palanāti Vīra Charitra, K.A.R.Y.C.*, p. 1708.
66. *C.T.I.*, Part II, No. 8, Vol. 13, Nalagālakōta, the son of Sabbasenni conquered the Kōtas and captured the city of Dharanikōta. For this feat he was honoured by his master Rudra with the title 'Koṭagelpāta' or the conqueror of Dharanikōta.
67. *S.I.I.*, Vol. X, No. 241, Tripurāntakam, d. 1185-6 A.D., *E.H.D.*, Part IX, p. 594.
68. Pālkuriki Sōmanada-*Panditarādya charitra*, E.H.D., Part IX, p. 593.
69. Kākatīya records *under* Rudra are last seen in the Gōdāvari delta in 1285-6 A.D., *S.I.I.*, Vol. IV, No. 1155.
70. *E.H.D.* Part VIII, The Yādavas of Śeunadēsa by Prof. A.S. Altekar, pp. 520, 525, and 531.
71. *Chaturvarga Chintāmani, Vratakhamda, Rājaprasasti* by Hemadri-*E.H.D.* by Bhandarkar, APP.C.V. 4; *E.H.D.* Part VIII, p. 529, Patan Ins. of Yadava Mahadeva, *E.I.* XXXII, p. 33.
72. Palampet Ins. of Rēcherla Rudra-*H.A.S.* 3.
73. Yenamadala Ins. *E.I.* III, p. 101, *Pratāpacharitramu*, pp. 40-41. Rajaravapaḍu grant—*E.I.* XVIII, p. 354, Vol. 16.
74. *E.H.D.* Part IX, pp. 598-99.

75. *H.A.S.* Vol.III, Vol. 24, *S.I.I.* Vol. IV, No. 1117; A.R. 261of 1893- Rēcherla Rudra's title "Kākatiya Rājya Bhara Dhanraya". "Kākatīya Rājya Sasmrtha" indicates his governing Kākatiya kingdom.
76. *E.I.* Vol. III, p. 111, Bhawal Ins. of Singhana dt. 1222-23 A.D. I.A. Vol. XIV, p. 316; Penthan Copper plate grant of Rāma Chandra dated 1271 A.D. the *Yādavas of Śeunadēsa* by Prof. A.S. Altekar, p. 530, *E.H.D.* Part VIII, *E.H.D.*, Part IX, pp. 598, 599 and 600.

2

Gaṇapatidēva on the Throne

The earliest record of Gaṇapatidēva is the Manthena epigraph dated 26th December, 1199[1] which seems to be his first regnal year. The circumstances under which of Gaṇapatidēva was set free and reinstallled on the throne by the Yādava king Jaitugi or Jaitrapala are not definitely konwn. The Śeuna inscriptions no doubt, attributed his regaining of freedom to the compassion felt for him by the Yadava ruler. Sympathy and generosity may indeed have played their part, but political considerations must also have weighed with the Yadava ruler in setting youthful captive at liberty. He probably desired to secure himself against an attack from the east in the event of conflict with the Hoysalas in the wrested from him a large part of the Northern Karnataka must have made him apprehensive regarding the safety of his southern frontier.

According to the Palampet inscription of Rēcherla Rudra datable to A.D.1213[2], after the death of Rudradeva, the nobles of the royal family and the enemy kings of the neighbouring states who probably did not approve the Mahadeva's succession rose in revolt. Among those enemies certain Nāgatirāja is stated to have been put to fight by the celebrated Kākatīya general. In the light of the Kukanūru plates Nāgatirāja was the younger brother of Bottu Kusūmāditya of the Mudigoṅḍa Chāḷukya family, the donor of the grant[3]. Although this charater is not dated, in view of the epigraph found in the Nattarāmēśvaram temple, Tanuku Taluk, dated A.D. 1218 which mentions both Kusumāditya and Bottu Nāgatirāja[4] it can be reasonably assigned to some time before A.D. 1213, the date of the Palampet inscription. We can therefore identify the enemy of the Kākatīya general mentioned in the Palampet record with Nāgatirāja, brother of Kusumāditya of the Mudigoṅḍa Chāḷukya family. They were ruling in those days Visurunāḍu, the Gōdāvari region of the present Khammaṁ district and their territory once extended upto Koravi in Warangal district. Kakati Rudra, it seems, in the last years of his career invaded Visurunāḍu and drove out these Chāḷukyan chiefs from their land, as one can gather from the Kukanaru plates which state that owing to certain calamities (bhu-praghattana) the brothers Kusumāditya and Nāgatirāja had to seek refuge in the territory of other kings. We have, therefore, sufficient reason to believe that soon after the death of Rudra they made an attempt to reassert their authority in the region upto Koravi which obviously led them to a conflict with the Kākatīyas.

Rēcherla Rudra inflicted a defeat on Nāgati and made him free and seek refuge in the Kolanu region as indicated by the Nattameśvaram epigraph dated A.D.1218. The victory of Rēcherla Rudra over Nāgatirāja seems to have taken place some time during the short reign of Mahadeva or soon after his death. Some schōlars hold the view that Kuḷōttunga Chōḍa III also invaded the Kākatīya kingdom. According to one of Kuḷōttunga's inscriptions, he subdued the Vadugus (Telugus) who were fierce in war and (thus) brought Vengai-mandalam under his sway[5]. Kuḷōttunga III effected his entry into Warangal by lavish bribery and gifts of gold. But Rēcherla Rudra, the commander-in-chief of the previous ruler, saved the kingdom from disintegration. He forsooth cut off the head of a haughty feudatory, and set it up for public view, stuck upon the top of the lofty flag-staff, in his lords city, that field for the harvest of prosperity, (as a scare-crow) to frighten the flocks of the wild beasts that are hostile kings[6]. But in the absence of proper evidence their view cannot be accepted at present. Rudra appears to have taken the administration of the kingdom into his own hands in the absence of his master for the titles Kākatīya-raja-bhāra-dhaurēya and Kakatīrājya- Samartha associated with his name clearly show that he carried on the administration in the name of his lord and sovereign Gaṇapatidēva.

The reign of Gaṇapatideva, though it began under unfavourable circumstances, was destined to become one of the most brilliant epochs in the history of the Āndhra country. Ganapati was an energetic monarch, almost the whole land inhabited by the Telugu speaking peoples was brought under his sway by war or diplomacy during his long reign of sixty-one years. His task of establishment of large kingdom became comparatively easy due to the political disintegration which followed the dismemberment of the western Chalukyan and Chōḷa empires. The Kākatīya kingdom was subjected to the authority of numerous petty chiefs engaged in constant internecine warfare for self-aggradizement. The chiefs of Velanāḍu demand attention first. Although their power declined after the death of Chōda II about A.D. 1181, Prithiśvara's authority over the northern portion of the maritime Āndhra country remained intact until the time of his death about A.D. 1210 which was indicated by the inscriptions at Srikūrmaṁ, Drāksharamaṁ and Piṭhapuraṁ[7].

At the moment when Gaṇapatidēva at length took the reigns of the government into his own hands the prevailing political conditions were as follows.

Some of the loyal subordinates of his family in the Divi island and its neighbourhood acknowledged his suzerainty and helped him in his wars[8], though ruling their own fiefs as independent princes. A tradition preserved in the Telugu *Simhasana-dvatrimsika* of Gōparāja, a work composed in the early 15th century A.D., represents Pṛithvīśvara as ruling from his ancestral capital Chandavolu in the Guntur district[9]. The evidence of the inscriptions, as well as literary tradition, thus bears testimony to the continuance of the rule of the Velanāti family over part, if not the whole of the coastal Āndhra country. Their authority such as it was; must have been limited by the power of numerous autonomous or semi-autonomous petty feudal states which honey-combed the country. The region around the Kolar lake was ruled by the chiefs of Kolanu or Sarasipuri. The Gudimetla Chāgis held sway over parts of the Kṛishna tract in the interior, and the Natavāḍis over the territory along the northern bank of the Kṛishna river now included in Khammaṁ district. Some parts of present Guntur region were governed by the Kotas; and Telugu Chōdas of Konidena and further south lay the Telugu Chōḷa kingdom of Nellōre, comprising the Nellore and Cuddapah districts of the Āndhra Pradesh, and the major portion of the Chingleput district of the Madras state with the cities of Nellore and Kānchi as alternate capitals. A small tract of territory at the junction of the Nellore, Guntur and Kurnool districts was ruled by the petty chief of Ēṛuva under the supramacy of the Nellore Chōlas, whilst several minor principalities flourished in the Guddapah and Kurnool marches. And the Gangas of Kaḷiṅga were supreme in the north-east of that country.

Conquest of Coastal Āndhra

The policy which Gaṇapatidēva had to follow in dealing with these states had already been marked out by his predecessors. Both Prōla II and Rudra had cherished imperial designs; they desired to bring under their rule not only Telingāṇa but also the coastal districts, and to establish their supremacy over the whole of the Āndhra country. They were completely successful in reducing of Telingāna but they failed in the conquest of the South and the East, owing largely to the opposition of the Valanāṭi chiefs who were then ruling the maritime tracts as the nominal representatives of the Chāḷukya-

Chōḷa emperors in the South. After consolidating his position in the capital, Gaṇapatidēva turned his attention to the coastal Āndhradeśa. At that time the power of the Velanāṭi chiefs, however declined after the death of Chōda II about A.D. 1181 and Pṛithvīśvara, Chōda II's grandson, appears at that time to have exercised some sort of authority over his ancestral kingdom; but he was not strong enough to check the turbulence of the nobility or to stem the forces of disintegration. The Velanāti king Pṛithvīśvara temporarily changed his capital from Chandravolu to Pithapuram and began to reassert his power in the Kṛishṇa region.

During these conditions, Gaṇapatidēva invaded the coastal districts with strong forces in the year A.D. 1201, accompanied by all the subordinate chiefs whom he could master, such as the Kolas, Natavāḍīs and Malyālas. He first attacked Bezwada which stood on the eastern frontier of the Kākatīya kingdom. The Bezwada epigraph of Natavāḍi Rudra, brother-in-law of Kakati Gaṇapatidēva dated A.D. 1201 indicates the beginning of the Kākatīya conquest of the region[10]. Bezwada was soon captured, and the invaders proceeded eastwards to the island of Divi, near the mouth of the Kṛishna, then the headquarters of the Ayya chiefs who held sway over the fertile tracts of the delta. Certain Pinna Chōḍi of the Ayya family was ruling this island probably owing allegiance to Velanāti Pṛithvīśvara. Some account of these Ayya chiefs is given in the Gaṇapēśvaram inscription of Jāya-Sēnāpati dated A.D.1231[11]. The Ayya chief did not submit without stubborn resistance. Entrenching themselves to the strong fortifications of their island fortress, they stoutly opposed the advance of the invaders but were finally obliged to surrender and to see their rich and beautiful capital plundered by the enemy. A description of the conquest of this island is given in the Konḍaparti inscription of Malyāla Chauṁḍa dated A.D.1203. In recognition of the meritorious services rendered by the Malyāla chief Chaumḍa, Gaṇapati conferred on him, as stated in the Kondaparti inscription dated Śaka 1125 (A.D. 1203), the title of Dvipilumtaka or Divi-Chūrākāra that is the plunderer of the island of Dvipi or Divi[12]. Gaṇapati did not annex the conquered territory to his kingdom, for he was an astute politician and understood that by adopting a policy of concilliation he would be able to build up his power on permannent foundations. He therefore dealt leniently with the vanquished Ayya chiefs. He not only restored their possessions but contracted matrimonial relations with them by marrying Nārāmba and Pērāmba, the two daughters of Ayya Pina Chōḍi. Having been impressed by the good qualities of young Jāyapa, son of Pina Chōḍi, Ganapati took him into his service and got him well trained in state craft and commanding of elephant forces. As a consequence of these victories not only Divi but also the whole of Velanāḍu, as is in fact stated in the Ganapatiśvaram inscription dated A.D. 1211, fell into the hands of Gaṇapatidēva at this time.

Consequent on Ganapati's occupation of Divi and Velanāḍu what happened to Pṛithvīśvara in not clearly known. But from the provenance of his inscriptions in the Kaḷiṅga the territory between Dāksharāma in the East Gōdāvari district and Śrīkūrmam in Śrikukulam district was actually under his sway. However in order to recover his lost position in Velanāḍu he seems to have launched an attack on the Kākatīya subordinates. Gaṇapatidēva met the enemy on the battle field with forces gathered from all resources. Among others who joined the Kākatīya forces Tikkabhūpāla, the Chōḍa king of Nellore[13] and certain Mahamaśalesvara Ballayya of Kammanadu[14] were the most prominent. The Velanāti Pṛithvīśvara was slain in the battle. Gaṇapatidēva in some of the inscriptions is praised as Pṛithvīśvara-śirah-kanḍuka-krīdāvinōda, the player of the ball that is the head of Pṛithvīśvara.[15] Similarly Tikkabhūpāla was eulogised with the same title. The last date of Pṛitivīśvara as noticed in the Śrīkūrmam inscription of his chief treasurer Ananta[16]. being A.D.1206, his demise in a battle with the Kākatīya king may be assigned roughly to some time after that year. Gaṇapatidēva appointed Jāyapa-Sēnāpati as the governor of Velanāḍu country in A.D. 1213, the date of his Chēbrōlu inscription[17]. His Chandavolu inscription is unfortunately partly built in a wall[18] and we do not know if it contains an earlier date. The inscription in the Chennakēśava temple at Idupulapāḍu in the Bapatla Taluk dated A.D.1209 is the earliest record of Gaṇapatidēva in this region which signifies his complete annexation of Karmmarashtra and Velanāḍu to the Kākatīya Kingdom[19] by that time.

Southern Expedition

Gaṇapatidēva began to interest himself in the affairs of the Southern kingdom very early in his reign. The Chēbrōlu inscription of Jaya-Sēnāpati dated Saka 1135 (A.D.1213) alludes to an expedition against the kings of the southern region which Gaṇapati had undertaken on an earlier occasion[20]. The conquest of the Southern kings and the expansion of the Kākatīya power in that direction were the direct outcome of his alliance with the Telugu Chōlas of Nellore who had established themselves there during the first half of the 12th century A.D. Nalla Siddhi had become the master of a compact state comprising the modern Nellore, Cuddapah and Chingleput districts together with the prosperous cities of Nellore and Kānchi which served him as alternate capitals. Due to the weakness of Rajādhirāja II, the successors of Nella Siddhi, seem to have asserted their independence. Very little is known about the events of the reigns of Beta I and Eṛra Siddhi I, who succeeded him on the throne. Eṛra Siddhi had three sons, Manuma Siddhi I, Beta II and Tammu Siddhi. Of these, the eldest, Manuma Siddhi I, followed him on the throne. During the reign of Manuma Siddhi I, Kulōttunga III invaded the Telugu Chōḷa kingdom in order to bring it back under his suzeranity. As the inscriptions dated in Kuḷōttunga III's third regnal year (A.D.1180) are found in Kānchi, Nanḍalur and Kālahasti[21] all then included in the kingdom of Nellore, the campaign against the kings of the North and the entry into the city of Kānchi must have taken place at this time. It was obviously directed against Manuma Siddhi I, who seems to have forfeited his throne as a consequence of his defeat. The victorious Chōḷa king Manuma Siddhi's younger brother entrusted the kingdom to Manuma Siddhi's younger brother Nalla Siddhi and returned to his capital in triumph. Nalla Siddhi's inscriptions ranging in date from A.D. 1187 to 1204, found scattered in various localities within the Nellore kingdom, show that he remained loyal to his Chōḷa king.[22] Subsequently the government passed into the hands of his younger brother Tammu Siddhi, who seems to have usurped the throne and held it until A.D.1207-8. Tikkabhūpāla, the son of Manuma Siddhi I, who considered himself to be the rightful heir to the throne, solicited Ganapati's help to regain his patrimony. Tikka helped for this Gaṇapatidēva in the war against Pṛithvīśvara. In return for this help, Gaṇapati, after reducing Valanāḍu to submission, marched against Nellore and having put its ruler Tammu Siddhi and his supporters to fight[23], installed Tikka on his ancestral throne and returned home as stated in the Chēbrōlu inscription cited above, by way of Tāmrapuri.

Tikka was indeed an able and warlike Prince; but owing to the aggressions of powerful neighbours he was not infrequently hard put to defend his frontiers and preserved the integrity of his kingdom. It was probably for this reason that he propitiated Kulottunga III by acknowledging his supramcy,[24] though he had himself come to power with the help of the Kākati Gaṇapatidēva by ousting his uncle, who was himself a loyal feudatory of Chōḷa emperor. Tikka had to face, early in his reign, the Śeunas who invaded the Nellore kingdom to destroy the power of Tikka; following this he lost Kānchi and his other possessions in the Tamil country as a result of the political disorders prevailing there, though he acknowledged the supremacy of the Chōḷa king Kuḷōttunga III, and kept on friendly relations with him. Between A.D. 1215 and 1228 the total absence of any inscriptions of Tikka seems to indicate that during these years he had again been driven from the throne. Tikka, according to contemporary Telugu literature and the Telugu Chōḷa inscription is said to have vanquished his enemies single handed by his own efforts without any help from allies. Tikka defeated the Śeuna army in the battle fought at Kurumulur in the Cuddapah district and made prisoners of all their horsemen[25]. There is reason to believe, however, that Tikka actually owed his success, atleast in part, if not wholly, to the help sent to him by Ganapati. In an inscription of Mattewaḍa in the Warangal district dated A.D.1228, Gaṇapati is said to have plundered a Chōla capital probably Kānchi[25]. The later Gaṇapēśvaram inscription of Jayapa-Sēnāni dated A.D.1231, in which it is stated that Gaṇapati, having easily subdued the Chōla, the Kaḷiṅga, the Śeuna, the Bṛihat-Karanataka and the Lata made the whole country of Velanāḍu his own together with Dvīpa[27]. It may be noted that all the kings mentioned here, excepting the Lata, were rulers in South India. Evidently Tikkabhūpāla had to face a combination of the kings mentioned above; and he naturally seems to have sought help from his old friend Ganapati. It was under these circumstances that Gaṇapati proceeded to the South at the head of his army and having defeated and driven out the associated kings he restored Tikka at Nellore and Kānchi. Tikka appears to have appointed, in this context, the Kāyastha

Ganagaya Sāhīni, a brother-in-law of Ambadeva I, one of Ganapati's vassals, as the Governor of upper Pākanāḍu to strengthen his position in the interior of his kingdom. Tikka's troubles, however, were by no means at an end. His interests clashed with those of the Hoysalas; and he was soon involved in a war with them.

Tikkana Sōmayaji's statement in the introduction to *Nirvachanōttara Rāmayanam* indicates that Tikka by inflicting a defeat on Karnata Someśvara established his own power and having without difficulty restored the Chōla to his throne, assumed his (Sōmēśvara's) title of Chōḷa-Sthpanāchārya 'the establisher of Chōlas'. This clearly shows that he had embarked on the war on behalf of Chōla king Rājarāja III. The details of this war are not known, but it is clear that Tikka marched to the South at the head of his army and killled Narasimha II in battle at Jambai in A.D.1239, defeated in the next year Narasimha's son Somesvara who had attacked him to avenge the death of his father, and assumed the title of Chōla-Sthapanacharya, which he bore thereafter. We have at present no information to show whether Tikka received any help from Gaṇapati in his war with the Hoysalas. It is not, however, unlikely that Gaṇapatidēva took part in this conflict also, for the Hoysalas, who were then in the heyday of their power, could hardly have been defeated by the unaided efforts of a minor chief like Tikka. Of course, there is as yet no evidence and in the absence of authentic information, the entire credit for the victory must be ascribed to the prowess of Tikka himself.

Kaḷiṅga Expedition

After his victory over Pṛithvīśvara, Gaṇapati naturally designed to bring the latter's possessions in Kaḷiṅga under his rule. He therefore sent an army into that country to reduce it to subjection. The conquest of the coastal districts to the east of Warangal, including the powerful principality Kolanu (Sarasi-

or-Kamatakapuri) was partially accomplished. He sent an army under the command of Sōmamantri of the Indulūri family who was one of the ministers of Gaṇapatidēva[27] and Rajamayaka the general of Rēcherla Rudra. According to the Upparapalli inscription of Kātināyaka son of Rājanāyaka dated A.D.1236, the later was credited with millitary victories at Bokkera, killing the chief bearing the title Gōdhumarati capture of Udyayagiri and putting to flight certain Padiraya[29], Bokkera is identified with a place of that name in the Aska Taluk of the Ganjam district. The identity of Gōdhumarati in not known. Jāyapa Sēnāni in his Gaṇapēśvaram inscription was also credited with the slaying of this chief bearing the title Vairi-Gadhuma-Gharōtta, the crushing stone of wheat like enemies[30]. Even such a warrior, it is said, became the first prey to the sword of Jāyapa Sēnāni. As this indicates Jāyapa's earliest military undertaking, the event must have taken place before A.D.1213, the date of his earliest record at Chebrolu[31]. Udayagiri which is identified with the place of that name in Pedakimidi agency is said to have been captured by Rājanāyaka. The identity of Pedaraya is not known. Having accomplished these victories, the Kākatīya general visited the Bhīmēśvara temple at Drakshārāma and endowed it with a perpetual lamp in Saka 1134 (A.D.1212)[32]. According to *Śivayogasara*, a Telugu work by Kolani Gaṇapati of 15th century, one of his ancestors named Śomā-mantri, having conquered Gōgulanāḍu and Kolani-viḍu, crossed the Gōdāvari and captured the two Māḍiyas and the twelve Manniyas and occupied the land of Kaḷiṅga-Sīma.[33]

Thus it is evident that the Kākatīya forces during this campaign penetrated into Kaḷiṅga as far as Aska in the Ganjam district. The Kaḷiṅga king Anaṅga Bhīma III who succeeded his father Rājarāja III in A.D.1211 seems to have not only freed his country before long from the Kākatīya occupation but also penetrated into the south as far as Dakshārāma. An inscription in the Bhīmēśvara temple dated in his eighth regnal year, A.D. 1217-8 states that he had effected the deliverance of his country Trayīvasuṁdhara or Trikaliṅga[34]. Gaṇapati's expedition against Kaḷiṅga was no doubt a brilliant demonstration of his military strength; but it did not fetch him any material benefit. On the other hand, there is reason to believe that the Kākatīya forces suffered a defeat at the hands of the Gaṅga king Anaṅga Bhīma III and were forced to retreat to the south of the Gōdāvari. Not only that, Aniyaṅka Bhīma extended his influence into the Vēṅgi country also.

Kammanāḍu

The Kammanāḍu affairs demanded immediate attention of Gaṇapatidēva. Some of the Chiefs in the districts, probably Telugu Chōḷas of Koṇidena, appear to have defied Gaṇapati's authrority and began to rule as independent ruleres, Opill Siddhi, a scion of the Pattapi branch of the Telugu Chōḷa family, was commissioned by Ganapati to reduce them to obedience and to bring the entire district under his control. Ōpili Siddhi accomplished the task to the entire satisfaction of his master and obtained Governorship of the territory from him as a reward for his services[35]. The Chakranārāyaṇa princes who were ruling over Addanki and its neighbourhood seem to have been conquered about the same time. The provenance of Ganapati's numerous inscriptions leaves no room for doubt that this region also passed into his hands before A.D.1217-18[36].

Conquest of Kolanu

This region was ruled by the Kolanu chiefs who had their headquarters at Kolanu or Sarasipuri (likely to be Saripella) in the West Gōdāvari district. Mahamanḍalēśvara Kolani Kēśavadēva, who came to the throne in A.D.1192, held sway over the country for thirty-six years until A.D.1228[37]. It was probably after the death of that chief that Aniyanka Bhīma III considering that the time was now propitious for realizing his long cherished desire, resolved to attempt the subjugation of Vēṅgi. The Kākatīya armies were at that time busy in the south waging war against the Hoysalas and other southern rulers on behalf of the Telugu Chōḷa Tikka of Nellore. In order to ensure the success of his attempt; Aniyaṅka Bhīma appear to have espoused the cause of the Velanāti Chief's Kulottuṅga Rājēndra Chōḍa and Gonka, descendants of Velanāti Pṛithveśvara, and to have despatched his army to effect the final conquest of Vēṅgi. Jasrojaka, the son of Khadgasimha, the Commander-in-chief of his forces, arrived in A.D. 1230 at Drāksharāmaṁ, where he busied himself with carrying out repairs to the temple of the God Bhīmēśvara. His arrival at Drāksharamaṁ was in fact the prelude to the outbreak of the war; during the next three years he was fully engaged in accomplishing his object[36].

Gaṇapatidēva did not remain silent to the aggressive activities of the Kaḷiṅga king. As soon as he installed Tikka in Kānchi in A.D.1228, he recalled his army from the South and concerted measures for the expulsion of the Kaḷiṅgas from Vēṅgi and for bringing that country under his sway. He sent an army under Indulūri Sōma-mantri and Ēṛuva Bhīma, Kalapa Nāyaka and Malyāla-Hēmādri Reddi who seem to have accompanied him and rendered him valuable assistance. A study of the sites of the Kākatīya inscriptions shows that the process of the conquest began as early as A.D.1231. An epigraph of Ganapati engraved on a pillar in the temple of Pāliśvara at Iragavaram in the West Gōdāvari district dated A.D.1231 shows that Kolanu was conquered by him in that year[39]. Velanāti Coṅka who suffered a defeat at the hands of Malyāla Hēmādri Reddi took to fight[40]. The two inscriptions of Aniyanka Bhīma datable to A.D.1230 and 1223 found at Drāksharāma indicate his hold over the region atleast on the northern side of Gōdāvari[41]. In one of these records the commander of the Ganga army Jasrojaka is credited with the conquest of Vēṅgi in no time (druta-jita-vislasad-Veṅgimaṇḍalēna) which indicates that the Ganga forces were active in Vēṅgi at that time. It is not known whether the Ganga general actually conquered the Vēṅgi country or simply rendered military assistance to the Kolani chief to repel the Kākatīya incursion. There is no positive evidence to prove that the Kākatīya king could establish his authority in Vēṅgi before A.D.1240. The reference to Ganapati's conquest of Kaḷiṅga, noticed in the Ganapēśvaram, Upparapalli and Mōtupalli inscriptions no doubt indicates his attempt to subjugate Kaḷiṅga and Vengi country right from, A.D. 1212 but they did not fetch him any material benefit. Conquest of the Kolanu region by Indulūru Sōma-mantri might have taken place some time before A.D.1240, that is after the death of Kolanu Kēsavadēva Mahārāja whose inscriptions are not noticeable upto A.D.1231[42], and the retreat of the Ganga forces. The provenance of the inscription of the Kākatīya general Malyāla Hēmādri Reddi dated A.D.1237, in the Draksharāma temple supports this view[43]. And it is quite probable that in order to secure political allegiance of the Chāḷukyas of Nidadavolu, Gaṇapati entered into marital alliance with those chiefs by offering his daughter Rudrama to the Chāḷukya prince Virabhadra.

The Eastern Ganga attacks on the Kākatīya dominions did not however, cease with Ananga Bhīma's death, for his son and successor, Narasimha-I who ascended the throne in A.D. 1238, followed his father's aggressive policy. In the *Vallabhābhyudayamu,* a late Telugu rendering of the Sanskrit *Srīkākula Mahātmam,* the Sthalapurānam of Srīkākulam in Kṛishṇa district, it is stated that Narasimha sent a military expedition against Kānchi under the command of his foster brother, Danḍanāyaka Anantapāla, and that the latter halted at Srikakulam during his march to erect a temple to the God

Telugu Vạllabha (Āndhra Vishnu), and then proceeded to Kānchi, where after defeating his enemies and exacting tribute from them he set-up a pillar of victory describing his exploits and then returned home in triumph[44]. No record of Anatapāla has so far been discovered; therefore the information furnished by the Sthala-purānam cannot be verified at present.

The Kaḷiṅga expedition of the Kākatīya alluded to in the Nandalūru inscription of the Telugu Chōḍa king Manuma Siddhi-II dated A.D. 1257 must have been a later incident when the Kākatīya had to defend themselves against the invasion of the Ganga king, Narasimhadēva-I. Here also it is stated simply that Manuma siddhi crossing Gōdāvari chased the king of Kaḷiṅga into his territory, which indicates that the Kākatīya could not seize any territory beyond Gōdāvari[45]. This incident might have taken place some time after the accession of Manuma Siddhi-II in A.D.1248.

Second Southern Expedition

The state of affairs in the South underwent a sudden change with the death of Tikkabhūpāla in A.D.1248. The affairs of Nellore which were again in chaos called for Gaṇapati's intervention. On the death of Tikka the succession to the throne of Nellore was in dispute. The principal claimants were Tikka's son Manuma Siddhi-II and a certain Vijaya Ganda Gōpala, who claimed himself to be scion of the Telugu Chōḍa family and seized the Southern part of the kingdom of Nellore comprising the present Chingelput and North Arcot districts. Only the Northern part comprising the present Nallore and Cuddapah districts remained under the control of the rightful king Manuma Siddhi-II, son of Tikka. To strengthen his position Vijaya Ganda Gōpala entered into an alliance with the kings of Dravida and Karnataka. The former was no doubt the Chōḷa monarch, Rājarāja II or his co-regent Rajendra III, who had been recognized as heir-apparent to the Chōla throne in A.D.

1246 and had since then been virtual ruler of all the Chōla territory. The Karnataka was certainly Vira Sōmēśvara (A.D.1234-5-60). Through he was assisted in the administration of his Karnataka and Tamil possessions by his two sons Narasimha III and Vira Ramanatha respectively, he yet wielded supreme power over his entire kingdom until the very end of his reign. Sōmēśvara must have welcomed the professed allegiance of Vijayaganda Gōpala, as it gave him an opportunity to re-establish his rule over Kānchi and its neighbourhood. Having thus strengthened himself, Vijaya Ganda Gōpala appear to have made an attempt to extend his authority northwards into the Nellore district[46]. At the same time in Nellore a rebellion headed by the Padiharis Bayyana and Tikkana broke out against Manuma Siddhi-II and drove him out of his capital. A Vaidumba chief named Tikkarasa Ganga alias Rakkasa Ganga occupied Manuma Siddhi's territory in the Cuddapah district defeating Gangaya Sāhini, the commander of Manuma Siddhi's forces and ousted him from his governorship and annexed his territories[47]. Manuma Siddhi-II thus became, as a consequence of a combination of circumstances which he could not control, a king without a kingdom. He therefore appealed to Gaṇapatidēva for help. His loyal minister, the famous Telugu poet Tikkana, the celebrated auther of *Āndhra Mahabhārata* was sent as emissary to Gaṇapati's court.

He was warmly received at the Kākatīya court. Realizing the gravity of the situation with which he could not remain unconcerned, Gaṇapatidēva despatched a powerful army under Samanta Bhoja to the South. He personally marched to Nellore to reinstate Manuma Siddhi on his ancestral throne. According to the undated Nayanapalli inscription in Guntur district,[48] the Kākatīya army reduced Nellore to ashes, played a game of ball with the heads of the Padiharis Bayyana and Tikkana and having entered the Dravidamandala captured, perhaps Kānchi the capital of Kulōttunga Rājēndra Chōḍa. Kuḷōttunga Rājēndra mentioned in the record seems to have been Rajendra III who was taking active part in the administration of the Chōḷa kingdom since A.D.1246. Sāmanta Bhōja fought a decisive battle at Palaiyaru in the Tanjore district, against the combined forces of Drāvida, Karnataka and Vijaya Ganda Gōpala and captured Kaṅchi in A.D. 1250. But the provenance of Vijaya Ganda Gopala's inscriptions in Kānchi till A.D.1282 indicates that Manuma Siddhi failed to re-establish his power in Kānchi though he did so in the Nellore region.

Gaṇapatidēva in Western Āndhra

The victory obtained in the battle of Palaiyaru and the capture of Kānchi by Samanta Bhoja in A.D.1250 do not seem to have produced any permanent results, because the provenance of Vijaya Ganda Gopala's inscriptions leaves no room for doubt that he soon recovered his hold over Kānchi and its neighbourhood, and continued to rule there until A.D.1282[49]. What enabled him to regain his power without difficulty was doubtless the pre-occupation of Manuma Siddhi II and Ganapati with the affairs of the Western Telugu country. Rakkasa Ganga as may be remembered, defeated Gangaya Sāhīni, the Kāyastha chief, whom Chōḍa Tikka had appointed as the commander of his forces in Upper-Pakanadu, and had seized the territory under his rule. He was supported in this attempt by the Telugu Chōḍa Chief of Jagatapi-Gutti (the modern Gutti in the Anantapur district) who, as a consequence, assumed the title of 'Gandapendera-Gangayasa-Sarvasva-bandikara' or the plunderer of the entire property of Gandapendera-Gangaya Sāhīni. Ganapati and Manuma Siddhi after their victorious campaign in the Tamil country, marched against him by way of Kalahasti in the Chittoor district and attacked him there. In the war that followed Rakkasa Ganga was worsted and had to surrender the territories which he wrested from Gangaya Sāhīni. Though Tikkana attributes the credit for the victory to the powers of his master Manuma Siddhi, the evidence of the inscription clearly shows that it was not achieved without the Kākatīya support. Gangaya Sāhīni, after his defeat at the hands of Rakkasa Ganga and his consequet loss of terrıtory, joined the service of Ganapati, who conferred on him the high office of baha-Hara-niyog-adhipati (the Superintendent of the 72 niyogas) at his court[50]. This fact is recorded in one of the inscription at Tripurantakam dated A.D.1250. Gandapendera Jarnigadeva, a nephew of Gangaya Sāhīni and a feudatory of Ganapati and subsequently of Rudrama evidently assisted his uncle in the campaign against Rakkasha Ganga. Ganapati also conferred on Gangaya Sahini the region of Marjavadi, part of the territory which he conquered from the Vaidumba Chief Rakkasa Ganga, as a family estate[51].

Ganapati's Relations with Śeunas

The relations between Gaṇapatidēva and his western neighbours the Śeunas were normally amicable throughout his long reign of sixty-one years. Gaṇapatidēva gave asylum to the Śeuna princes and appointed them in his service. Certain Permadideva, son of Singhana is noticed in an inscription dated A.D.1159 at Peruru in Nalgonda district where he is stated to have made gifts of lands to Brahmins all over the country ruled by Gaṇapatidēva. In this southern compaign against the Pandyas, Gaṇapatidēva was assisted by some Yadava chiefs as commanders of his forces.

Pandyan Invasion

Gaṇapatidēva's alliance with the Telugu Chōla kings of Nellore involved him in a war with the Pandyas of Madura, who under the able leadership of the famous Jatavarman Sundara Pandya-I, subjugated between A.D.1251 and 1257 the whole of Southern India and established their hegemony over it. As the Telugu Chōla rulers of Nellore owed allegiance, even though only nominally to the Chōla emperor, the Pandyas who had overthrown his authority considered that as his political successors they ought to bring the Telugu Chōla dominions also under their control. Of the two Telugu Chola chiefs who succeeded Tikka, his son Manuma Siddhi II, held the northern or Telugu districts whilst Vijaya Ganda Gopala ruled over the southern or Tamil districts. The latter by reason of the proximity of his territory to the Pandyan kingdom, and also on account of his alliance with the redoubtable Kadava chief; Kopperunjinga, naturally became the object of their first attack. Both of them not only surrendered themselves to the victor but also joined with him in attacking the Nellore kingdom. They next turned their attention to Nellore. Manuma Siddhi II apprehending the danger, immediately appealed to the Kākatīya king, the Śeunas and the Bana rulers for help. The provenance of the inscriptions of Rajendra Chōda III, Vijaya Ganda Gopala and Kopperunjinga, the vassals of the Pandyas at Tripurantakam[52] in the heart of the Kākatīya kingdom indicates that these dignitaries were commissioned by the Pandyas to penetrate into the Kākatīya territory. Kopperunjinga proceeded upto Draksharamam probably to establish contacts with the king of Kaliṅga, the enemy of the Kakatiya monarch.[53] The latter perhaps to bring about a split in the Pandyan camp and win over the Kadava chief to his side honoured him with the decoration of Vira-Pada-mudra (Presentation of the anklet of the heros)[54]. According to the Pandyan records, it is believed that while the expedition under Kopperunjinga was advancing towards the North, the main Pandyan army led by Jatavarman Sundara Pandya Bhuvanaika-vira Vikrama Pandya and Jatavarman Vira-Pandya captured Nellore and killed Manuma Siddhi II in a fierce engagement at Muttukuru in A.D.1263. His allies the Kākatīyas, the Śeunas and Banas were put to fight I[55]. The Telugu Chōla kingdom of Nellore and Kānchi were annexed to the Pandyan empire, though its administration was entrusted to the brothers of Manuma Siddhi II (also known as Vira-Ganda Gopala) who apparently were compelled to rule it as the vassals of the Pandyas[56]. In honour of his victory Jatavarman Sundara Pandya celebrated his *Virabhisheka* (anointment of conquest) at Nellore and Kānchi[57] and issued special coins bearing the symbol of the Kākatīya boar in the obverse besides the Pandyan emblem of the fishes on the reserve. This military defeat of Gaṇapatidēva coincided with his final retirement from the active politics of the kingdom.

Ganapati's Inter-State Relations

Ganapati is credited in several of his inscriptions with victory over the kings of several other countries. The Chēbrōlu inscription of Jāyapa, for instance, states that the Hammira, the Huna and the king of Kasi were suppliants at his door[58]. Similarly it is stated in the Pakhal inscription that his heralds at each assembly announce before him the names of the Lord of Kasi, the Saka monarch, the ruler of Kerala, the Lord of Kaḷiṅgas, the Huna king, the prince of the Kurus, the king of Tummana, the Lord of Arimarda, the ruler of the Nepala, the Magadhas, the Chōla monarchs and present them to him[59]. Ganapati's relations with the rulers of the Kaḷiṅga and Chōla countries have already been noticed. Of the other kingdom Madra, Panchala, Videha, Kashi, Magadha, Kuru, and Nepala were situated in the North; and all of them excepting probably the last disappeared long before the time of Ganapati, for the whole of Northern India was at the time under the rule of the Sultans of Delhi. The Saka rule which had been confined to western India in ancient times was destroyed by the Gupta emperor Chandragupta II, Vikramaditya in the latter half of the fourth century A.D., and the Hunas were overwhelmed by Yasovarman and Narasimha Gupta Baladitya early in the next century. Neither the Sakas nor the Hunas are known to have ruled subsequently in any part of India. The inclusion of the kings of these countries among the princes who came to pay homage to Ganapati must, therefore, be attributed to a literacy convention popular with the Prasasti writers of the period and it may be dismissed without serious consideration. Tummana was situated in the Madya Pradesh adjoining Telingāna and Kerala in the extreme south on the west coast. Arimarda has been identified with Pegu on the Burmese coast; it is not unlikely that Ganapati may have had intercourse, friendly or otherwise, with rulers of these countries.

Though begun under unfavourable circumstances, the reign of Ganapati was the most brilliant epoch in the history of Āndhra. At the time of his accession the Āndhra country was in a state of political disorder. The power of the Chāḷukya-Chōlas and the Chāḷukyas of Kalyani had finally disappeared, leaving behind several feudal states small and big engaged in constant wars for supremacy. He set before himself, the task of restoring political unity of the Telugu country either by war or diplomacy and he succeeded in a large measure in accomplishing this object.

An important event which rebounds to the credit of Ganapati was the change of the capital from Anumakonda to Orugallu. The foundations for the new capital were laid by his uncle Rudradeva in his last years. Ganapati continued his work, and built two forts one within the other, constructed respectively of stone and of mud. The new fort according to tradition was provided with seventy five bastions, the protection of each being entrusted to a nayaka in the service of the king.

Gaṇapatidēva had no male issue, but he had two daughters the elder Rudramba or Rudramadevi and the younger named Ganapamba or Ganapambadevi. The former was given in marriage to a prince of the Eastern Chāḷukya lineage called

Virabhadra, and the latter to Beta of the Kota family. Ganapati chose his elder daughter, Rudramadevi, as the heir apparent , and regarding her as a son, named her Rudradeva and in A.D.1260 or a little earlier made her his co-regent.

References

1. *I.A.P.*, Ka. 28.
2. *I.A.P.*, Wg. 50.
3. E.A. IV, pp.
4. *S.I.I.* Vol. X, No. 262.
5. Inscriptions of the Pudukkotta State, 163, 166, K.A.N. Sastri, *Cholas*, II, 125, 133, 142.
6. *H.A.S.*, III, Vol. 22.
7. *E.I.*, IV; pp. 32; *S.I.I.*, V, 1100; *Mack Mass.* 15-6-26; *Elliots Collections*, p. 133; No. 55; *A.R.E.*, 370-13 of 1896; S.I.I., Vol. 1254.
8. E.I. III, No. 15, Vol. 30, p. 87: Choda-Prithivisa-bhupasya-Chatur-asa-Jayavahah-abhuvan-bahu-viryyena-chatvaro-bhata-pungaboh.
9. Bharati, XXII, Part I, p. 546.
10. *E.I.* VI; No. 15; p. 159.
11. *E.I.* III, p. 91.
12. *C.T.I.*, Part II, Nos. 8 (v. 55) and 9 (v.53); Dr. P. Srinivasachari's translation 'even in heaven as Churakara' is absurd.
13. Tikkana Somayani, *Nirvachanottara Ramayana*, p. 132. Here-in-after referred to as *Nir-utta*.
14. *S.I.I.*, VI, 165.
15. P.V.P. Sastry, *Select Epigraphs of Andhra Pradesh*, p. 62.
16. *S.I.I.*, V, 1254.
17. *E.I.*, V, p. 142.
18. *SI.I.*, VI, 214.
19. *Ibid.*, X, 248.
20. *E.I.*, V, p. 149.
21. *A.R.E.* 403 of 1919, 195 of 1892, 556 of 1907.
22. *N.D.I.*, No. 40, 85; *A.R.E.*, 317 of 1929; 198 of 1892; 601 of 1961.
23. *Nir-utta* 133, *A.R.E.* 446 of 1920; *A.R.E.* 1920, II, para 55.

24. *N.D.I.*, R. 8.
25. *Nir-utta* I, 33, *A.R.E.* 446 of 1920; *A.R.E.* 1920, II, para 55.
26. *C.T.I.* Part II, No. 10.
27. *E.I.* III, p. 91.
28. *Kalinga Sanchika*, p. 382.
29. *I.A.P.* Kn. 30.
30. *E.I.* III, p. 88, Vol. 41, "Ya-vaiva-gōdhuma-gharatta-nāmma vyarājata prek-kabalas-sa-Jatah". Basing on the statement of the Tallaproduturu inscription some scholars opined that Ēruva Bhima joined the forces of Ganapati in the latter's Kalinga campaign (EHD; p. 606). But the statement in that inscription dated A.D. 1322, that Ēruva Bhima conquered several places in Vengi, Orissa and the Bastar state seems to allude to the events of still earlier period than Ganapati's reign. Ēruva Bhima joined the service of Kalyani Chalukyas and obtained Panugallu rajya as fief probably from Ahavamal Sōmēśvara I, who invaded Chakrakuta and Vengi passing through Manthena. This Eruva Bhima according to the Ollala inscription of his great grandson dated A.D. 1098 was the founder of the Kanduru Choda family (*E.A.* iv. pp. 55-58). Manthena was already included in Kakatiya Kingdom even before Ganapati's accession. Hence the need does capture by Eruva Bhima on Ganapati's behalf does not arise. The matter in the last verse of the Talla Prodduluru inscription seems to refer to Eruva Bhima of the Kanduru Chōda family.
31. *E.I.*, V. p. 143.
32. *S.I.I.* iv, 1117.
33. R.Subbarao (ed.)-*Kalingadesa charitra*, p. 382.
34. *S.I.I.*, Vol. IV, No. 1329.
35. *S.I.I.*, Vol. VI, 628 (*A.R.E.* 183 of 1899).
36. *N.D.I.* ii Ongole, 17, 45, iii, Ongole, 139.
37. *S.I.I.* IV, 181; *A.R.E.* 531 of 1893; 167, *A.R.E.* 527 of 1893; 175, *A.R.E.* 529 of 1893; X. 262, *A.R.E.* 723 of 1930; 268, *A.R.E.* 735 of 1920; IV. 187, *A.R.E.* 532 A of 1893.
38. *A.R.E.* 430 of 1893; *S.I.I.*, IV, 1252, *A.R.E.* 357 of 1893.
39. This inscription which has been copied by the late M. Somasekhara Sarma remains yet to be published.
40. *S.I.I.* IV, 1333, *A.R.E.* 283 of 1905.

41. *S.I.I.* Vol. 1360, 1252.
42. *S.I.I.* Vol. V, 187.
43. *Ibid,* Vol. IV, 1333.
44. Madras University, *Andhra Granthamala,* No. 8, pp. 63-65, 83-84.
45. *S.I.I.* Vol. V, No. 187.
46. *N.D.I.* iii, S.I. 8.
47. *Nir-utta* 1, 41.
48. *S.I.I.* X, 376.
49. *A.R.E.* 137 of 1916.
50. *S.I.I.* X, 332; *A.R.E.*, 283 of 1905.
51. Dr. N. Venkataramanayya, Perur Inscriptions No. 12.
52. *A.R.E.* 1905, Nos. 197, 198, 202 and 272.
53. *S.I.I.* XII, 247; *A.R.E.* 1905, No. 195.
54. *T.T.D.I.*, I, 19.
55. *A.R.E.* 1913, Nos. 332, 340, 354, 361 and 365.
56. K.A. Nilakanta Sastri, *The Pandya Kingdom*, p. 168.
57. *A.R.E.* 1914, Part II, para 18; *S.I.I.* IV, 865.
58. *E.I.*, V, p. 149.
59. H.A.S., No. 4, p. 10.

3

The Feudatories of the Empire

Gaṇapatidēva was assisted in his wars and in the administration of the kingdom by a large number of feudatories, generals, ministers and officials. All of them, to whichever category they belonged had to serve in the army, as the public services were organized on a military basis. It is not possible, to make any distinction between civil and military properly so called because no such distinction existed at that time. Their office was generally hereditary, inherited from their forefathers. They were the worshippers of the lotus feet of their sovereigns[1]. Among the feudatories, the capable and talented were chosen for royal services and were appointed to high offices of administrative and military authority. These feudatories were the means of contact between the sovereign and the people. To keep up the contact, Ganapati restored the old ruling families of the conquered regions, who inspired the loyalty of the local populace as feudatory ruleres. And when the unscrupulous among them exploited the situation and rebelled, he used force only to subdue, but not to destroy them.

The king never let any service go unrewarded. Every victory won by his officers was recognised and rewards and tittles were showered on each of them. In their turn, they respected their sovereign and served him loyally and tried to live up to the trust placed in them. Their contribution to the state was very significant.

It is curious feature in the Kākatīya royal family, that they never intermarried with any neighbouring great power, right from the beginning. Some plausible reason can be offered for this policy of isolation[2].

During the early stages, when the Kākatīyas were an infant power, their neighbours, the Yādavās, the Chōlas, the Hōysālās and the Pāndyas, claiming themselves to be Kshatriyas, probably did not wish to connect themselves matrimonially with an admittedly Śūdra family. The Kākatīyas power was not strong enough to relegate their birth to the background. An alliance with them would neither be a social upliftment nor a political advantage. Later on the Kākatīyas followed a policy of expansion, founded vast empire on their own strength, with numerous chiefs vanquished, but not all reconciled to their victories. To control them and if possible to win their willing loyalty into himself was of primary concern to the Kākatīyas monarch. And as a rising power the Kākatīyas had to establish themselves at home first. At this stage, among other measures, they followed a policy of marriage alliances with such chiefs as would serve to conciliate them and really their willing support for stabilising the Kākatīyas power in Telangāna, and for further expansion in future. By securing Natavāti Muppamāṁba as his queen.[3] Prola II enjoyed the support of the Natavātis in establishing himself an independent power.

His successor Rudra I, after defeating the Kandur Chōdas, conciliated them by marrying their princess Padma[4]. It is not known from which famillies Bayyāmba[5], the wife of Māhadēva and the mother of Gaṇapati, and Somamba[6], the wife of Gaṇapati and the mother of Rudramadēvi, came from. In all probability they must have come from some local ruling families, but certainly not from any powerful neighbouring royal house, for otherwise the fact would not have been ignored. Māhadēva following in the footsteps of his brother, married his two daughters, Kuntaladevi and Mailadevi to the two sons of Natavāti Buddha, called by the same name Rudra.

The Kākatīyas power was established by the time that Gaṇapatidēva came to the throne and it was left to Ganapati to expand it into an empire. He followed the old policy of conciliating the conquered. As conquests were chiefly in the coastal regions he allied himself with the people of those lands. The marriage of his sisters, Mailāmba and Kundāmba into the Natavāti family[7], helped him in his campaigns against the Velanāḍu chiefs[8].

The feudatories may be divided broadly into two classes, old and new. The Rēcherlas and the Malyālas were the oldest of the Kākatīya feudatories.

The Rēcherlas

The Rēcherlas ruled the modern Nalgonda district and were powerful feudatories during the time of Gaṇapati and his predecessor. Rudra, the head of the Rēcherla family, played an important role in the affairs of the Kākatīyas kingdom in the beginning years of Gaṇapatidēva's reign and saved it from destruction. When on the death of Kākati Rudra and his brother Māhadēva in the wars with the Seuṇas, and the imprisonment of Gaṇapati at Dēvagiri, the nobles rose in revolt and warriors from beyond the frontier swept the country, Rudra stood firmly loyal and took upon himself the tasks of preserving the integrity of the kingdom. He drove out the foreign invaders, put down the nobles with a stern hand, and governed the land until the return of his young master from captivity at Devagiri[9]. Rājānāyaka, the commander of Ganapati's forces, followed the Kākatīyas forces to Kaḷinga when, after the death of the Velanāṭi king Pṛithvīśvara, Gaṇapati invaded that country in A.D.1212, and rendered distinguished service on several fields of battle[10]. Several other members of the Rēcherla family are mentioned in the inscriptions but they do not demand any special notice, since they do not seem to have had any considerable share in the state affairs.

The Malyālas

The Malyālas ruled parts of the modern Mahaboobnagar district. In the reign of Gaṇapatidēva the ruling chieftain of this family was Chaumḍa, the son of Kāṭa. He was the conqueror of Kōṭa. He deserves particular mention for he took a leading part in the early wars of Gaṇapatidēva with the Velanāṭi ruler Pṛithvīśvara. The appellations dvipilumtaka and divi-chūrakāra which are associated with his name in the inscriptions clearly prove that he played an active role in the overthrow of the Ayya family and the subjugation of Divi which has situated on the shore of the estuary of the river Krishna[11].

Ayya Chiefs

Ayya chiefs ruled the island of Divi, near the mouth of the Krishṇa. After capturing Bezwada, Gaṇapati invaded Divi but they did not submit without stubborn resistance. Finally they surrendered to Gaṇapati. Gaṇapati did not annex the conquered torritory to his kingdom. He not only restored their possessions but contracted matrimonial relations with them by marrying Nārāmba and Pērāmba, the two daughters of Ayya Pina Chōḍa. He also took their brother Jāya or Jāyapa into his sevice. Jāyapa was a distinguished soldier who was specially skilled in training the war elephants and overseeing their employment on the field of battle. He became the gaja-Sāhini of Gaṇapati and rendered valuable service in his wars, especially during his campaign in Kaḷinga. Jāyapa was a connoisseur of art and a distinguished man of letters; he composed a treatise on dancing and Chareography called the *Nrittarafnavali,* which is considered by competent authorities to be the best work extent on the subject by any Indian writer.

The Telugu Chōlas of Nellore

Situated as the Telugu Chōḍa kingdom of Nellore was, on the southern fringes of the Kākatīya empire, it was bound to play a significant role in the political set up of the times. Theoretically the Telugu Chōḍas were the subordinates of the Chōḷas of Tanjore. But their allegiance was merely nominal, for the central Chōḷa power at this time, was on the wane both politically and militarily. The Telugu Chōḷas were more exercised by the dominating Kākatīya influence to their north, and had to trim their policies with an eye on the Kākatīyas reactions.

The arrival in Nellore of Kākatīyas Gaṇapati to help Chōḍa Tikka is an obvious indication of the increasing influence of the Kākatīyas in that region. Thenceforth whenever the Telugu Chōḍa rulers were in trouble, and appealed to the Kākatīyas, they unfailingly came to their rescue[12]. The Kākatīyas policy became one of waging wars for and along with the Telugu Chōḍas but never against them. Though the Telugu Chōḍas would off and on recollect their Chōḍa sovereign, they virtually became a subsidiary dynasty under the Kākatīyas. Tikka and Manuma Siddhi II played vital roles in the southern wars of Gaṇapatidēva.

The Ēṛuva Chiefs

How and when the Ēṛuva chiefs were reduced to subjection by Ganapati is not definitely known, but they appear to have come under the Kakatiya power soon after the overthrow of the Velanāḍus. It appears that Chōḷa Tikka undertook the conquest of the district ruled by the Ēṛuva chiefs, at the instance of Gaṇapatidēva. This conquest was effected before Ganapatis invasion of Kalinga in A.D.1212, for Ēṛuva Bhīma who must have entered into the service of the Kākatīyas monarch after the subjugation of his terrritory, took an active part in the Kalinga expedition.

The Pottapi Chiefs

The Telugu Chōlas of Pottapi appear to have come under the Kākatīyas rule about the same time or a little later. Ōpili

Siddhi of this family, at the instance of his master Gaṇapati, defeated Mallidēva, the Telugu Chōḷa of Koṇidena, conquered Kamma-nāḍu, and was granted possesion of the six thousand country as a reward for his services[13].

The Addanki Chiefs

The Chakranārāyaṇa princes of Addanki were probably forced to submit about the same time. Mahāmanḍalēśvara Mādhava Mahārāja of this family, who was apparently an independent chief in A.D.1208-9, is said in an inscription of his son Sārangadharadēva, dated 1254-5, to have been a vassal of Kākati Gaṇapati[14]. Ascertain Mādava or Mādhava Nāgaka, a subordinate of Gaṇapati, who was ruling this region in A.D. 1239-40, has been identified with this Mahāmandalēśvara Mādhava Mahārāja[15]. If this identification should be accepted, it would corroborate the evidence of Sārangadharadēva's inscription that Mādhava was indeed a vassal of Gaṇapatidēva. He was succeeded by his sons Singhaladēva and Sārangadharadēva, who ruled their principality jointly as the subordinates of Gaṇapatiḍēva until A.D.1257.[16] The Chakrānarāyaṇa line has been wrongly taken by modern writers to been an offshoot of the Śeuna family of Dēvagiri. There is however, absolutely no evidence in support of this view, though, as Mādhava Mahāraja and his descendants were members of the Śalankayana gōtra or clan, it is not improbable that they had some remote connection with the kings of the Śalankayana dynasty who held sway over the coastal Āndhra country in the fourth and fifth countries of the Christian era.

The Chāḷukyas of Nidaḍavōlu

The Chāḷukyas of Nidaḍavōlu who ruled the territory comprising the modern West Gōdāvari district gained importance as close relations of Kākatīya royal family. They claimed descent from Eastern Chāḷukyas. They do in fact figure in the inscriptions of Gaṇapatidēva, but nothing of importance is known about them though Ganapati's daughter Rudrama was given in marriage to Vīrabhadra, one of the members of the Chāḷukyas of Nidaḍavōlu[17]. Bhīmarāju another member of this family, made the gift of a village to the temple of Tripurāntakamāhadēva at Tripurāntakaṁ in A.D.1257. He took an active part in the southern expeditions of Gaṇapatidēva. His titles Dravilabhayajvara, Karṇāṭamāṇḍalika-vairi-gōdhūma-ghaṭṭana ghaṭṭa, and Belleḍerayadisapaṭṭa clearly indicate that he participated in Sāmanta Bhōja's expedition in 1249 A.D.[18]

Another Chāḷukya chief, whose name is now unfortunately lost, held the offices of the Sakala Sēnādhipati (commander-in-chief of all the armies) and Paṭṭasāhini.

The names of several generals in the service of Gaṇapatidēva are recorded in the inscription of his reign, but as no information is available about their careers or the part they played in the wars of Gaṇapatidēva, most of them do not call for special notice.

Sāmantabhōja

He belonged to Dōchi family. He led the Kākatīyas armies under Gaṇapatidēva in the southern expedition in 1249 A.D. He defeated the southern rulers and captured the city of Kānchi, where he re-established the authority of the Telugu Chōḷa king of Nellore. He also assisted Manuma Siddhi II and Gangaya Sāhini in over-throwing the Kalukaḍa chief Rakkasa Gaṅga.

Bhāskara or Bhāskaradēva was the commander of the elephant force. Prōlu Rautu was the tantrapāla or war minister[19]. There is no detailed information about them.

Ministers under Gaṇapatidēva

The Indulūri Family

They served the Kakatiyas since the days of Rudra I. Combining in themselves the Brahmin and Kshatriya qualities.

These Brahmin chiefs of the Kouṇḍinya gōtra[20], acted as ministers and generals. Kolani Gaṇapatidēva in his *Sivayogasāramu* gives a detailed account of this family describing them as great scholars, well-versed in all the Vedas and Śāstras.

The most illustrious among them was Sōmaya ranking as a Mahāpradhāna at the court of Gaṇapatidēva. If we can trust the evidence of the *Śivayōgasāra,* he commanded the Kākatīya expeditionary force against Kaḷinga in A.D.1212, when he overran that country, and having destroyed the authority of the Kolanu chiefs, reduced Vengi to subjection. In recognition of his meritorious services, Gaṇapatidēva seems to have conferred on him the title of Kolanisōma. He, like several others of his community, followed the profession of arms and by sheer merit rose to the position of one of the foremost generals in the service of his master Gaṇapatidēva. In this way they helped Gaṇapatidēva in extending the Kākatīyas kingdom, northwards into the land of the Kaḷingas, and eastwards into the basin of the Gōdāvari and the Krishṇa[21].

Prōla Bhīma Nāyaka

Another illustrious Mahāpradhāna was Prōla Bhīma Nāyaka, who bore several distinguished titles, the most important of which was Āruvēla-dūshaka (destroyer of the Āruvēlu, i.e., the Velanāḍu six-thousand country), Sūryavaṁśa-pratishthāpanāchārya (the establisher of the solar family of kings). As Prōla Bhīma Nāyaka is said to have died in A.D.1213, it may be presumed that he served in Ganapati's last war on Pṛithvīśvara of Valanāḍu, in which he restored Chōḷa Tikka of Nellore to his ancestral kingdom, and helped this prince to reconquer the city of Kānchi from his enemies[22]. Muchināyaka of the Musundiri-anvaya, and Penungula vaṁśa and Manuma-kula, who had the title 'Kānchipura Nirjīta-Jayānaganā-Vallabha', i.e., the lord of the lady victory won by conquering the city of Kānchi[23] appears to have assisted Prōla-Bhīma Nāyaka in recapturing Kānchi.

Pōtana, Kūchenapreggaḍa, and Konḍaya Preggada all held office under Ganapatidēva as Pradhānas.

Gangava Sāhini

The more important among the feudatories of the Kākatīyas were the Kāyastas of Mulikināḍu. They ruled over the provinces on the southern borders of the Kākatīya empire. It was their homeland. The Kākatīya power over these areas could not be stable without their unfailing alligiance. They were great cavaliers and generals and shaped the political events of these days to a large extent.

On their part, the Kāyasthas realised that, alone they would be nowhere, sandwiched as they were between the Kākatīyas, the Yādava, the Hoysāla and the Pāndyan powers. Their talents would flower only under the shelter of one of these powers which then shared South India. This protection was offered by the Kākatīyas around 1250 A.D.[24] when Gangaya Sāhini left the services of the Telugu Chōḍas of Nellore to become the *bahattara niyōgādhipati* of Gaṇapatidēva[25] i.e., the superintendent of the seventy-two categories of royal services in which the Sōnādhyakshas, Mahāpradhānās, Pradhanas, etc. were included, but whether he actually occupied such an important place at Ganapati's court cannot be ascertained definitely, as the evidence on the subject is so meagre and fragmentary. Apart from his role as a *bahattara niyōgādhipati,* Gangaya Sāhiṇi was a distinguished military officer, he was probably in-charge of the Kākatīyas cavalry, for he is spoken of, in one of the Tripurāntakaṁ inscriptions as a turaga-sadhanika.[26] The early History of Gangaya Sāhiṇi is obscure. According to the Kaifiyat of Oguru, he was originally in the service of Chōḍa Tikka of Nellore.

who appointed him as the governor of his territories above the Eastern ghats[27]. On the death of his master in A.D. 1248, he was attacked by the Kalukāḍa chief Rakkasa Ganga who deprived him of his authority and drove him into exile. Thereupon he entered the service of Gaṇapati about A.D. 1250, probably with the help of his brother-in-law Ambadēva, and succeeded some time before A.D. 1253 in winning back his territory. Gaṇapatidēva appointed him to the office of the bahattara niyōgādhipati, as stated already, and conferred on him an extensive tract of territory extending from Pānagallun in the Nalagonda district to Mārjavāḍi which he ruled from Vallūru-paṭṭaṇa in the Cuddapah district as his capital[28]. It may be noted here that this territory granted by Gaṇapati to Gangaya Sāhiṇi as his fief became the nucleus of the short-lived Kāyastha kingdom of Vallur which rose to considerable power under his successors. Gangaya Sāhiṇi is said in his inscriptions to have won victories over several enemies of whom, however, nothing more than their name is now known to us. He died in 1257 A.D. after serving Gaṇapatidēva for eight years. As he had no issue, he was succeeded by his nephew Jannigadēva, the son of his younger sister Chandaḷadēvi. Gangaya Sāhiṇi had in his service an able minister called Nāmadēva Panḍita, who helped him to carry on the administration of his territory. He (Gangaya Sāhiṇi) stood high in the favour of Gaṇapatidēva, who granted to him the standard of mūrurāya-jagaḍāla and the title Chālamartiganda.[29]

References

1. *N.D.I.* Vol. I, d. 59 Potlapadu record of Tripurari, D. 1272 A.D. *S.I.I.* Vol. X, No. 422 Durgi Insc. of Janniga, D. 1269 A.D.

2. The Kākatīyas marriage alliances are more elaborately discussed

by M. Pratibha in Appendix No. 2 entitled "The Kākatīyas Matrimonial Policy' of her unpublished Ph.D. thesis 'Kakati Rudradevi' submitted to Andhra University.

3. Bayyaram grant—*Bharati*, April, 1967.
4. Anumakonda Insc. of Rudra, *I.A.* Vol. XI.
5. Bayyaram grant.
6. *Prataparudra Yasobhushanam*—*Kak. San.* App. 1.
7. Bayyaram Insc., *Bharati*, 1967 April, p. 2 Ed. by Sri P.V.P. Sastry, *S.I.I.*, Vol. X, No. 254, Tripurāntakaṁ.
8. *E.I.*, Vol. VI. No. 15, p. 159, The Bezwada Insc. of Natavāti chief Rudra, D. 1201 A.D.
9. *H.A.S.*, No. 3, p. 9.
10. *H.A.S.*, No. 3, p. 9; *S.I.I.*, IV, 1117.
11. C.T.I. Part II, Nos. 8, 9.
12. *E.H.D.*, Part IX, p. 610.
13. *A.R.E.* 183 of 1899; *S.I.I.*, VI, 628; *A.R.E.* 243 of 1899; *S.I.I.*, VI. 206.
14. *N.D.I.*, iii, 0.76; *N.D.I.* i, p. 17.
15. *N.D.I.*, iii, p. 1452.
16. *N.D.I.*, iii, p. 1451.
17. *S.I.I.*, X, 360; *A.R.E.* 740 of 1920.
18. *A.R.E.* 203 of 1905; *S.I.I.*, X, 355.
19. *A.R.E.*, 1929-30, para 30; *A.R.E.*, 1916, para 52.
20. *Sivavogasaramu*, Vol. 18, *Ka. San.*, App. p. 12.
21. *Sivavogasaram*, Vol. 25, and 26–M. Somasekhara Sarma, Kakatiyulu Kalingam '*Kalinga Sanchika*,' p. 381.
22. *A.R.E.* 1929-30, para 30.
23. *A.R.E.*, No. 188 of 1917; *S.I.I.*, X, 265.
24. *A.R.E.*, 283 of 1905, Tripurāntakaṁ, D. 1250 A.D., Record of Gangaya Sāhini for Ganapati's merit.
25. *A.R.E.*, 283 of 1905; *S.I.I.*, Vol. X, No. 332; *E.H.D.*, Part IX, p. 611.
26. *A.R.E.*, No. 268 of 1905; *S.I.I.*, X, 465.
27. Ch. Vīrabhadra Rao–*Kākatīya Andhra Raja Yuga Charitra*, p. 402.
28. *S.I.I.*, Vol. X, No. 422.
29. *A.R.E.*, Nos. 231 and 283 of 1905 and *S.I.I.*, X:, 332 and 343.

4

Administration and Military Organisation

The administrative pattern under Ganapati can be inferred from his inscription and those of his officials and subordinates. Though they yield valuable information we cannot take them on their face value. The above information could be supplemented by what can be culled out from the contemporary and near contemporary works on *rājanīti* like the *Purushārthasāramu* of Śivadēvayya, the *Nītisarāmu* of Pratāparudra, the *Nītiśāstra-muktāvali* of Baddena, and the *Sakalanītisammatamu* of Maḍiki Singana[1].

These works on Rājanīti are more diffuse in character based as they are on the ancient texts on polity, and the information they furnish, applies to a pattern of administration evolved through the ages. That these works came to be written in Telugu clearly indicate that the principles of state-craft enunciated there were evolved through the ages and could serve as guidelines intended for the Kākatīyas. Some of the authors like Śivadēvayya and Baddena lived and held important administrative offices under Ganapatideva.

Though the works, *Purushārthasāramu* and *Nītisarāmu*[2], are now extinct, the information and knowledge on Kākatīya polity and administration, are preserved for posterity by Maḍiki Singana in his *Sakalanītisammatamu.*

Administration

Though the monarch was the supreme head of the state with unlimited powers yet he did not behave like an autocrat.

As in the case of all Hindu kings, the power of the Kākatīya sovereign was subject to the limitations imposed by the dharma or the ancient custom of the land. The king could make no law as the 'sacred laws are coeval with the social organisation and are above him'. As the head of the administration, he was the support of the law and 'was only to obey and execute them'. He was only one of the seven constituent elements of the state; the saptāngas, which were the swami (king), amātya (minister), dēśa (territory), durga (fort), Kōśa (treasury), daṇḍa (army) and mitra (the ally) and not outside it, though his position among them was the most important. Thus theoretically he was no autocrat. The autonomy which the Samantas enjoyed, the position of the ministers whose advice the king generally sought, the powers of age long institutions having great influence locally such as craft-guilds, etc. and the possibility of an open rebellion by his people, or passive resistance by their migration from his kingdom in case of misrule all of these formed effective political checks on royal absolutism[3].

The monarch preserved and regulated dharma on which the social organisation and the well being of the society depended. Dharma included maintenance and proper administration of justice, maintenance of the social order, the varṇāśrama dharma, protection of the religion by building temples and giving grants to institutions or persons and the moulding of society to keep peace with the spirit and tendencies of the age. The last would be achieved by changing, modifying or amending the secular laws which were based upon the customs and usages of the people[4]. As a true Hindu sovereign Gaṇapatidēva sought smooth functioning of the varṇāśrama dharma, by protecting the Brahmins and establishing peace and security. Feudatory chiefs and subordinates vied with one anther to emulate their sovereign in observing varṇāśrama dharma.

Rājanīti lays down many qualifications for a king[5]. He must be well versed in the Vedas and Sastras and proficient in political science and fine arts. He must be wise, kind and just and treat his subjects as his own children. He should be kind and considerate towards his servants and dependants. He should use his power of discretion while choosing his subordinates for even if he is gentle and considerate in his behaviour, his wicked subordinates may make him inaccessible to the grievances of the people. To hear and redress the grievances of his people the king should grant them frequent audiences. Such and many more high qualities were required to make a king great, who would know no defeat[6].

Ministers

The king was assisted by in his administration by a number of ministers and officers. The minister occupied a vital position being one of the saptāṅgas of the state. At the time of choosing a minister the Rājanīti urges a very careful approach for a king. "The king must prefer a wise and trustworthy person who is discrete and loyal and should avoid fickle-minded individuals who are likely to divulge the secrets of the council."[7] Yet when the people and the king's own relatives approach him, the king should not always direct them to the preggaḍa or pregaḍa (minister). He should show himself as the real preggaḍa, and the actual preggaḍa as but his deputy[8]. The king should prevent the subordinates from growing as powerful and wealthy as himself for that would keep the king's position safe for a long time[9].

The king Ganapatidēva appointed a number of chief ministers which indicates his awareness of the danger of having a singleman entrusted with vast powers. The inscriptions and the contemporary Telugu literature mention many Mahāpradhānas, Pradhānas, Amātyas, Mantris, and Preggaḍas. But their actual functions and respective status in the official heirarchy are not clear. Some of the ministers not only assisted the king in his administration and offered advice on all matters of the state but also led armies into the battle-fields and governed parts of the empire as viceroys.

The rājanīti stresses that, brahmins of high intellectual capacities and scholarly attainments be appointed ministers, but the Kākatīyas made no communal distinctions where merit was cocerned[10]. The appointment of a minister was generally accompanied by the conferment of special honors and insignia, like the white or coloured umbrella, the palanquir, the viñjāmara fans, presents of valuable ornaments and costly perfumes together with titles of merit and a special court dress and a grant of vṛitti (land) pertaining to that niyōga.[11]

The Kākatīya ministers appear to have constituted a council of ministers and the monarchs used to deliberate and discuss with them daily all matters of state[12]. But the number of ministers is not known. Approximately there was the institution of the tīrthas, a group of eighteen ministers, like mantrin, Purōhita, mantri-jan-ādhyaksha, Sainyādhinayaka, āṭavika, prasastries, Sannidhātri, āyadha (āyudha), nāyaka, Samahartri, vyavahārika, danḍapala, prāntapāla, durgapāla, pradeshtri, karmantika, dairvarika, antarvaṁśikādhikāra and yuvarāja[13]. But as the contemporary inscriptions mention only few of above, it is difficult to reach at the exact number of the ministers in existence. These ministers were entrusted with specific functions, functions funamental to the running of the administration. There must have been ministers attending to them solely or in addition to their other functions. Inscriptions mention one Peda Mallaya Pregaḍa who served Gaṇapatidēva throughout his reign[14].

All officials, both military and civil and the royal household were classified under various niyōgas which were seventy-two in number, collectivly known as bahattara.

Bahattara niyōgādhipati was superintending over all these niyōgas. The Kākatīyas inherited this institution from the Western Chāḷukyas of Kalyani, where they had served. The Western Chāḷukyas themselves had inherited this office from the Eastern Chāḷukyas. In the reign of Amma-I of the Eastern Chāḷukyan dynasty (922-929 A.D.) appear a Niyōgadhikari[15]. By the time of the Western Chāḷukyas the niyōgas should have grown into 72, earning for the superintending officer the title of bahattara niyōgādhipati. The designation niyōgādhipati was the 'fore-runner of the bahattara niyōgādhipati of the later Western Chāḷukya times[16]. But the precise functions of the bahattara niyōgādhipati are not clearly spelt out.

Bahattara niyōgādhipatis in Gaṇapatidēva's time

This office appears to have been entrusted only to a mahāpradhāna or a feudatory. Apart from the Kākatīya monarch, even temple establishments had their own seventy two niyōgas. One such temple was the Tripurāntakaṁ temple at Tripurāntakaṁ[17]. Full details about the classification and functions of this office are not forthcoming in any of the evidence.

Inscriptions mention some other officers; they were "Sarvādhikāri" like Kurapati Surareḍḍi, who had a grant to the temple of Tripurāntakēśvara at Tripurāntakaṁ in the sixty-first regnal year of Gaṇapatidēva[18]. A certain Kamminayaḍu appear as the Rakshadhīśvara (governor) of Tadnuru[19]. A designation called 'dhānyādhipa' is known from a record from Malkāpuram. Dhānyādhipa was in charge of the grain department. The Telugu equivalent appears to be 'Koṭṭaruvu' which finds mention in the record. A certain Mallaya Preggada, the son of Kommana Preggada who belonged to the Bhāradvāja gōtra was the dhānyādhipa of Viśvēśvara Dēśika[20].

Territorial Divisions of Administration

The boundaries of Gaṇapatidēva's empire were Kalinga

on the North, Bay of Bengal on the East, Potḷacheṛuvu (modern Pattancheru) on the West and Kānchi in the South.

This extensive empire had its own territorial organisation for administrative conveniences. A full and accurate description is difficult as information is scanty.

The basic administrative division was the village. A group of village made a sthala, ranging from ten to sixty. Among them there were the Manuru sthala comprising of twelve villages[21], the Kondūru sthala consisting of eighteen[22], the Pallinādu-Gurindala[23] sthala made up of sixty villages. Records refer to some other sthalas, without specifying the number of villages under them. Such sthalas were Guruḍala, Piṁgali, Tangenḍa, Indulavāya, Ādara, Kōvuru, Kāvilasaṁkōta, Dhandrūru, Addanki[24], etc. A few records mention an analogous subdivision called Kampana[25]. There was another division called Sīma like Ganḍikōṭa Sīma[26]. Inscriptions refer to a few vishayas. A vishaya appear to have been a larger unit; they were Konnalivāḍi vishya, Hanumakonda Vishaya, Naṭavādi Vishaya[27]. Prof. Hultzsch translates the word vishayas to mean a district.

A 'nāḍu' consisted of several sthalas. The nāḍus of twenty-three nāḍus such as Hanumakonḍa nāḍu, Ayijanāḍu Kannāḍu, Karnāḍu, Kammanāḍu, Kamduranāḍu, Konḍapalli nāḍu, Kuśala nāḍu, Visuri nāḍu, Vēngi nāḍu, Vela nāḍu, Golula nāḍu, Gonḍa nāḍu, Merata nāḍu, Muliki nāḍu, Mingala nāḍu, Rāka nāḍu, Palli nāḍu, Pūngi nāḍu, Pottāpi nāḍu, Pulugula nāḍu and Rēnāḍu are known[28]. Epigraphs mention some nāḍus and vāḍis as vishyas too, as in evidence by Anumakonḍa nāḍu called Anumakonda-vishya and Velanāḍu called Velanāḍu vishya, and Natavāḍi mentioned as Natavāḍi vishaya[29]. The other territorial divisions were the vāḍi and bhūmi, like Mārja (mahārāja) vāḍi or Mārjavāḍa, Molta-vāḍi or Moltavāḍa, Arebhūmi and Nāgathala bhūmi[30]. The vāḍi was a survival from the past. The bhūmi occurs more frequently in the succeeding period[31].

Inscriptions mention provinces like Penabadi, Sakali, Ēṛuva or Ēṛavakali, Bhīrajati and some others like Ghanḍikōta, Peḍakallu, Nagārjunakōta Dharanikōṭa, who appear to have taken their names from the important cities and forts situated within their respective urisdictions.[32]

Villages were of two kinds, tax paid villages and the other one tax-exempted villages. Tax-exempted villages comprised the villages granted to temples or brahmins as Sarvamānya[33]. Irrespective of this distinction all the villages were under the administration of a body of village officials called collectively as 'āyagārs'. When it originated and when it supplanted the village assemblies is not known, but it was already well established during the Kākatīya period. The term 'ayam' means 'dimension', extent or measure as of a field. The āyagāras, therefore, denote people who held 'āyams' or fields of certain extent granted to them free of tax by the villagers or by the state as payment for undertaking public services[34]. Their names differed from localities to locality, they were twelve or more in number, the Karaṇam, Pedakāpu, Talāri, Purōhit, Goldsmith, Carpenters, Potter, Blacksmith, Washerman, Barber, Shoe-maker and Veṭṭi. In some villages there was the Nīrukattu, who was the waterman.

The Karaṇam had to keep the measurement or the extent and maintain the accounts of cultivable and non-cultivable lands, waste-lands, wet and dry lands, gardens and grazing pastures. Usually Karaṇams were brahmins and some of the Karaṇmas mentioned in the inscriptions of this period are; Annipeddi and Śrīkaraṇādhipati (probably superior officer) Nāmadēva Panḍita[35]. The Peda-kāpu or the Reḍḍi, was the village headman and tax-collector. Pedakāpu assisted the Karaṇam in the administration of the village. The village policeman was the Talāri, the village priest was the Purōhit, the Goldsmith, the Carpenter and the Blacksmith, the Potter, the Barber, the Shoe-maker and the Washerman attended to their respective duties in the village. The tank-bund was watched by the Veṭṭi or Water-man. The villagers provided grain called 'meras' to the āyagārs. The cultivators used to measure out to each of them a quantity of the produce for every field, Kapita or Heṁduga as fixed by custom of the village. Except the Karaṇam, Reḍḍi and Talāri, the āyagārs were primarily village officers and had little to do with the state. In the tax free villages like the dēvadāya and brahmadēya villages even they were exemped from paying taxes, but, instead of serving the state, they served the mahājana-sabhas of the agrahāras, the sthānikas and the committees of management in the dēvadēyas. The āyagārs 'served as a link between the village-folk and the government.'[36]

A sthala or nāḍu was probably governed by the sthala-karaṇams. The *Nītisāramu* of Pratāparudra mentions jānapadas governed by adhikāris of ministerial rank appointed by the king.[37] Probably the nāḍus were also called Jānapadas. The king directly appointed the adhikāris.

Military Organisation

Defence: Forts

Gaṇapatidēva devoted much of his energies to safeguard himself from external and internal enemies.

As defence demanded the building of forts it is consequential that much of the work on polity should be devoted building of the forts and the ways of strengthening them. Even though the king himself is a Ravana in valour he needs a fort, strong as Lanka fortified by the Sea, mountains and remparts.[38] And without such a stronghold even a powerful ruler would be an easy prey to his enemies.[39] If he strengthens himself with a network of forts rendering it difficult for the enemies to enter, his empire, will endure for a long time.[40]

There were three or four kinds of forts—the Sthala, the Jala, the Vana and the Parvatadurgas (Giridugas). The Sthala durga is a fort built on the plains. Water surrounds the Jaladurga, and forests envelop the Vanāḍurga. Those that were built on the top or slopes of a hill were known as Giridurgas. Yet even these should be fortified to render them unassailable.[41]

The empire of Ganapati was studded with these four types of forts. He had Jaladurgas like Divi and Kolanu, Vanāḍurgas like Kandūr and Nārāyaṇavanamu, Giridurga like Anumakonḍa and Ganḍikōṭa and Raichur.

All the four categories of forts should have special altalakas (rooms) over the Gōpuras (towers) wherein are placed various intricate machines of warfare guarded by well-trained soldiers. The forts should have sufficient fodder, for the livestock, besides fuel[42], oil, ghee, salt[43] and water. To facilitate the free-movements of large bodies of men, inside the fort there should be vast open places and they should at the same time provide for the free entrance and exit of the people[44]. There should be strict vigilance over the defiles, gorges and passes of the neighbouring hills. These forts should be well garrisoned with army placed at strategic places of the fort. The gates should be guarded day and night with caution. Guards should be posted at the central hall of audience, sentries should patrol around the palace and the talavaries (the watchmen) should go about in the streets and lanes.

Life in the army camp should be carefully supervised and there should not be any scope for any type of discontent. Torch bearers should go around constantly at night. The feudatory chiefs, captains and the soldiers should be treated with proper respect.[45]

Ēkaśila was beautiful and adorned with gardens and orchards containing variety of shady and fruit bearing trees.

They kept the city cool and during war they supplied fresh fruits and vegetables to the beseiged city.

The Army

The impregnability and unassailability of the fortress would depend on the army defending it. An army is traditionally divided into four categories of elephants, cavalry, chariots and infantry,[46] of them the chariots as a fighting corps had long been in disuse.[47]

Elephants

Elephants used to be imported from Ceylon, Burma and Pegu and partly captured in the forests and trained to be docile. They were kept in elephant stables and fed with palmirah leaves, rice and jaggery. They were bathed in nearby tanks and rivers and their faces were painted with vermillion and armoured with faceplates. These elephants not only used to bear generals on their backs but also participated in war.[48] The Gaja Sāhiṇis appear to have been the commanders of the Kākatīya elephantry,[48] and Jāyapa, the Gaja Sāhiṇi of Gaṇapatidēva, appears to have been specially skilled in training the war elephants and supervising their proper employment on the field of battle.[50] But the number of elephants that Gaṇapatidēva possessed is not known. Generals like Rēcherla Rudra had great capacity in protecting the Kākatīya kingdom from external and internal disturbances during the time of Ganapati's imprisonment by Yādava ruler. Of the Malyāla family, Chanḍa, took a leading part in the early wards of Gaṇapati with the Velanāṭi ruler Pṛithivīśvara.

Cavalry

Cavalry was another important division of the army. As horses were not bred anywhere in South India, they were brought from Sind, Persia and other countries, and were trained for the purpose of war. Warriors like Gangaya Sāhiṇi,

Jannigadēva and others seem to have shown a great interest in training the horses. Officers called the turaga Sādhanikas and aśvasāhiṇis appear to have been in command of the cavalry.[51]

Infantry

As there were continous wars on one border or another, and as there were no communal restrictions for military services, all men who are desirous to join the army were welcome. Even brahmin ministers like the members of Indulūri family shed their natural gentleness to take up arms and enter the battle fields. The Padasāhiṇi is probably in command of the infantry[52]. There is no evidence to know "whether the practice of drilling the foot-soldiers and instructing them how to combine mass movements on the battle field was known at the time"[53]. But all the warriors seeking military profession were trained in the gymnasia to wield various types of weapons like the sword the buckler, the lance and the bow.

Apart from infantry there were battalions of lancers. The entire Kākatīya army consisted of both the royal forces and the feudal levies, though it was not definitely known in what way they were officered and commanded.

Probably the Paṭṭa Sāhiṇis[54] were in-charge of the royal forces and the respective feudal chiefs led their own levies when commissioned by Gaṇapati. Dr. N. Venkataramanayya and Sri M.S. Sarma think that the officer Paṭṭa Sāhiṇi was attached to the royal establishment. But the Sāhinis appear to be military officers. The Gajasāhiṇi and the Asva Sāhiṇi and the Peda Sāhiṇi were in command of the elephantry, the cavalry and the infantry respectively. As the word 'paṭṭa' indicates royalty and as there were the imperial armies alongside the feudal levies, the word Paṭṭa Sāhiṇi must rerfer more appropriately to the head of the King's own forces.

The feudal levies or the nāyaka levies were the forces maintained by the nāyakas or sāmantas, for the service of the sovereign. These military chiefs were granted estates called the nāyaka-sthalas or the nāyaka sthala vṛittis for their up-keep and 'for the proper discharge of the duties pertaining to their office'. This nāyakara system was a heritage, bequethed by the Kākatīyas to the Rāyas of Vijayanagar who later handed it down to the nāyaks of Madhura. Under Kākatīyas its character and the political and military obligation are not precisely defined.

The Nītisāra states that villages were under the tutelage of the Sāmantas and the bigger ones reserved for the maintenance of the four-fold army and the replenishment of the treasury.[55]

Even the villages which the nāyakas held as feudal vassals were of two classes—small and large. The former was granted to them in lieu of salary, and the later for maintaining a stipulated body of troops, elephants, horse and foot and for paying an yearly tribute to the royal treasury. The sovereign had to maintain a stronger army than any of his feudal vassals to keep them in check. The system of checks and balances and the policy of keeping the nayak as constantly on the move from one place to another, removed the opportunity for these chiefs from becoming dangerously powerful[56]. There were about seventy-five nāyakas under Gaṇapatidēva.

Inscriptions mention military commanders like Danḍādhipathis, Sēnādhipatis, and Vatrinīpatis. The Sakala Sēnādhipatis were probably the chiefs in command of all the Kākatīya forces. Gaṇapati himself led the armies to the battle field as did his predecessors. He was accompanied usually by his angarakshakas who were his bodyguards. Besides them were a body of Leṅkas or companions at arms, who fought by the side of their sovereign. These Leṅkas took an oath that their Lord was their guru and deity in this world and the next. Disregarding wealth, comfort and even life they would stand by their Lord in his hour of danger and perish with him if it is necessary[57]. For a Lenka 'truth should be his utterance, praise (of his master) his work, charity his recreation, succour of the distressed seeking his protection his merit and unflinching courage in battle[57]. These duties and responsibilities of a Leṅka were known as the Leṅkavāti and the Leṅkas had estates granted by the king for their maintenance. The feudatory chiefs followed the example of their sovereign and had their own Leṅkas under them, so that these retainers became a common feature of Āndhra society during the middle ages.[59]

References

1. Verses from First there works are compiled by Madiki Singana in his *Sakalanitisammatamu* which has in addition, poems composed by him as well–*Sakalanitasammatamu*–edited by M. Ramakrishna Kavi, M.A.– "*The Forgotten Poets Series*", No. X (Andhra Patrika Publication, 1923).
2. The author of Nitisaramu is Rudra–I according to M. Ramakrishna kavi and Prataparudra according to Dr. N. Venkata Ramanayya and Sri M.S. Sarma–Sakalanitisammatamu, Edited by M. Ramakrishna Kavi "The Forgotten Poets Series", No. X; *E.H.D.*, Part IX, pp. 666, 707.
3. *South Indian Polity*–Kingship, pp. 17-21.
4. *Ibid.*, pp. 22-30.
5. *Purusharthasaramu*, p. 187; *Kamandakamu*, pp. 153-54.
6. *Sakalanitisammatamu*, v. 229.
7. *E.H.D.*, Part IX, p. 672.
8. *Baddenaniti–Sakalanitisammatamu*, Vol. 172.
9. *Ibid*, Vol. 174.
10. The cases of men like Malaya Hemadri Reddi and Muppidinayaka who were maha-pradhanas under Ganapati and Prataparudra respectively prove that no office had any communal restrictions. *A.R.E.*, 441 of 1893, *S.I.I.*, Vol. IV, No. 1333.

11. *Sivayogasaramu–Ka. San.* App. X, Vol. 461; *E.H.D.*, Part IX, p. 673.
12. *Purushārthasāramu–Sakalanitisammatamu*, Vol. 143.
13. *Sakalanitisammatamu*–2 : 373–*Kamandakamu*. Though the author gives the number of the tirthas as 21, he names only 18 listed above. *E.H.D.*, Part IX, p. 673.
14. *S.I.I.*, Vol. X, No. 369 'Sriman maha pradhani bahattaraniyōgādhipati–Induluri Gannaya; 1259 A.D. Tripurantakam.
15. *S.I.I.*, Vol. I, No. 36.
16. *E.H.D.*, Part IX.
17. *S.I.I.*, Vol. X, Nos. 465, 473; D. 1290 and 1292 A.D. respectively.
18. *S.I.I.*, Vol. X, No. 368, Tripurantakam; A.R.E. 220 of 1905-A.D.; 1259 A.D.
19. *Ibid.*, No. 402, Karempudi, Palnad Taluk, Guntur Dt., D. 1264 A.D.
20. *S.I.I.*, Vol. X; No. 453; Malkapuram, Guntur Taluk, Guntur Dt., 1282 A.D.; *A.R.E.* 98 of 1917.
21. *C.T.I.*, II, No. 53.
22. *S.I.I.*, Vol. X, No. 521.
23. *A.R.E.*, 307 of 1934-35
24. *S.I.I.*, Vol. X; No. 409; 488 and 500, 495, 504, 505; *C.T.I.*, II Nos. 54 and 34.
25. *S.I.I.*, Vol. X, No. 332 and 343.
26. *Ka. San.*, p.87; L.R., V.S. 9, 3 & 4.
27. *E.I.* Vol. III, Venamadala Ins. Tel. Ins. Vol. II, No. 1; *C.T.I.*, II, No. 7, *S.I.I.*, Vol. X, No. 254.
28. *E.H.D.* Part IX; p. 674; *S.I.I.* Vol. X; Nos. 442, 504, 371, 503, 504; Sivayogasaramu, *S.I.I.* Vol. X, Nos. 504, 334, 355, 448;

    E.H.D. Part. IX, p. 674. These two names are not to be found in the records that are cited as sources in the footnote in *E.H.D.* Part IX, p. 674.
29. *S.I.I.*, Vol. X, No. 442; *C.T.I.* Part II, No. 7; *S.I.I.*, Vol. X, Nos. 26 and 215, 322 and 254.
30. *S.I.I.*, Vol. X, No. 334 and 422, 346, 432, 504.
31. *E.H.D.*, Part. IX, p. 675.
32. *S.I.I.*, Vol. X, No. 525, 334, 504.
33. Vide Glossary *C.T.I.* Part II, Sarvamanya land exempt from tax.

34. *E.H.D.* Part IX, p. 675–Ayam means income. In this above interpretation ayam means the income of a land as remuneration.
35. *S.I.I.*, Vol. X, No. 422, 402, 334.
36. *E.H.D.* Part IX, p. 676; *Andhra Patrika*, Ugadi Sanchika, 1922, p. 157.
37. *Sakalanitisammatamu*–1, 203.
38. Purusharthasaramu–Sakalanitisammatamu, Vol. 51.
39. *Ibid*, Vol. 50.
40. *Nitisaramu, Ibid*, Vol. 53.
41. *Ibid.*
42. *Nitisaramu–Sakalanitisammatamu*, Vol. 53.
43. *Purushārthasāramu–Ibid.*, Vols. 58, 59.
44. *Nitisaramu–Ibid.*, Vol. 53.
45. *Ibid.*, Vol. 60.
46. *Nitisaramu–Sakalanitisammatamu*, Vols. 61, 62.
47. *South Indian Polity* by Dr. T.V. Mahalingam, p. 250; *E.H.D.* Part IX, p. 669.
48. South Indian Polity, pp. 252-53.
49. Dr. N. Venkataramanayya and Sri. M.S. Sarma think that the existence of the offices of the Gaja–Sahini and the Asvasahini indicates that the practice was in vogue of training both elephants and horses for the purpose of war–*E.H.D.*, Vol. X, p. 669.
50. *E.H.D.* Part IX, p. 616.
51. *A.R.E.*, 268 of 1905.
52. *S.I.I.*, Vol. X, No. 398.
53. *E.H.D.* Part IX, p. 669.
54. *S.I.I.*, Vol. X, No. 421.
55. *Nitisaramu–Sakalanitisammatamu*, Vol. 248.
56. M. Pratibha—*Kakati Rudradevi*, Cha. IV—"The Pillars of the Empire, p. 123. (Unpublished Ph.D thesis submitted to the Andhra University).
57. JOR, Vol. XIV, p. 109–There is no evidence of the lenkas in the Telugu land to have destroyed themselves after the death of their master. Whereas the garudas (who were of a similar category) under the Hoysalas appear to have immplated themselves after the death of their master (*E.C.* V.B.I., 112; *E.H.D.*, p. 670).
58. *A.R.E.* 443 of 1914; *S.I.I.* Vol. IX, No. 101 dated 1045 A.D.
59. *E.H.D.*, p. 670.

5

Social Conditions

An attempt is made hereunder to sketch the social conditions during the Kākatīya period, in general and during the reign of Gaṇapatidēva in particular. The general description of the social conditions during the Kākatīya period as a whole applies to the long reign of Gaṇapatidēva spreading over a period of more than sixty years (A.D.1199-1262).

In the Kākatīya period society continued to be organised on the basis of caste with all its hierarchial characteristics the Brahmin at the top, the Chanḍāla at the bottom and the Kshatriya, the Vaisya and the Śūdra coming in between. "Society is always a complex problem and more complex in the pattern of Hindu society"[1]. Sources are meagre and it is not easy to give detailed picture of the society of a bygone age. Only the outlines can be attempted as distinctions among various castes did not lead to social exclusiveness. A harmonious blending was attempted at the highest circles to weld the society into one united whole. The story of Jaina and Buddhist persecution by Gaṇapati hardly reflects the true social experience of his reign[2]. In fact the epigraphs reveal the conscious efforts of Gaṇapatidēva to unify the various sections and diminish the differences that existed within the different strata of society. The Rājguru himself instituted a feeding house where the hungry irrespective of their caste were fed[3].

The Brahmin

The Brahmin occupied the highest position in society under this system. The Brahmins continued to be the custodians of the Vēdas, the Śāstras and other branches of Vedic learning.

It was thus scholarship much more than his worth that brought to him the supreme position which he occupied. Educated men generally command respect in society and in medieval times, Brahmins were the only class of highly educated people.

The primary function of the Brahmin was a offer sacrifices to Gods, to officiate at such sacrifices to learn the Vedas and to teach the Vēdas. They also served as priests at all religious functions. Kings, noblemen and several other prominent men in society had Brahmins as their priests. Many held positions as priests in the numerous temple in the Kākatīya kingdom. Priests were known as purōhits. We have frequent references to such purōhits in the literary works of the period. Many others found vocation as accountants or Karanams at temples and villages respectively. Those who were well versed in the various branches of learning lived to propagate their knowledge and were aided by the rulers with grants of agraharas.[4]

For the performance of any important function—a marriage, a religious ceremony etc. it was necessary to fix an auspicious day and for this a knowledge of Pañchānga or Calendar was required. It was only Brahmins that possessed such knowledge and their services were needed for fixing such days[5].

The Brahmins did not constitute a homogeneous caste. They were divided into numerous sub-castes and each of these formed an exclusive group by itself; exclusive mean intermarriages and inter-dining between these sub-caste were not practised. The difference between one sub-caste and another was due to various factors. One such factor was the particular form of Hindustan which they followed. On this basis some came under the category of Smarthas who followed the Smrithis and worshipped both Siva and Vishnu. Some were Vaishnavites—the worshippers only of Vishnu and some were Saivites—the worshippers of only Siva.

Among the Saivites, the Aradhyas occupied an important place during this period. They worshipped Siva and proclaimed his superiority. The Ārādhyas also belonged to Gōtras like Vṛisha, Bhṛingi, Vīra and Skandha, which were not recognised as Gōtras according to Vēdas and Smṛitis. There were extremists among the Ārādhyas who condemned out-right the Brahmins of other sub-castes. Sōmanātha, the author of Basava Purāṇa and Panditārādhya Charitra was such a fanatic. He refused to recognise the non-Saivite brahmins as Brahmin. He referred them as Malas (the untouchables). He proclaimed that if any follower of Siva had contact with them he would be sharing their sins.

There were again sub-divisions among the Brahmins, depending upon the Vēda and the Śākha to which they belonged, their gōtra and the Nāḍu or territorial division which was their original home. Many of them were followers of Yajur-Vēda and belonged to the Yajus-śākha. The sub-divisions among Brahmins based on territorial difference was of a later-date and groups like Kammanāṭi Brahmins, Velanāṭi Brahmins, Mulikinati Brahmins originated in this way.

Another factor which led to the differentiation between Brahmin sub-sects was the profession which they followed. Brahmins served kings as ministers, generals, accountants and clerks. As a result of a large number of Brahmins taking to secular occupations like these, the sub-sect of Niyōgis came into existence during this period. Niyōgis (meaning assignees) were Brahmins who primarily took to service under rulers. The Niyogi Brahmins who were in the service of kings called themselves Amātyas. Amātya originally meant a minister.

Difference among some of the sub-sects arose as a result of the regions from which they originally migrated to Āndhra. There was a migration of several families from the South. Some of them settled in the rich and fertile delta of the Godavari.

Some of them settled in Bapatla, Kammanāḍu and their neighbourhood.

Another factor which led to the division of Brahmins into sub-sects was the particular region or Nadu in which they lived. Such were Pākanāḍu Brahmins, Mulikināḍu Brahmins, etc.

The agrahara was the home of the scholars devoted to learning and intellectual pursuits. A scholar who was a master in one or more śāstras or vēdas, was granted a whole agrahāra as ēkabhōgam or some vrittis in it. King Kākati Gaṇapatidēva gave on the auspicious occasion of a solar eclipse, the village of Kōlavennu situated on the banks of the river Krishna to 130 Brahmins. This inscription says that 'King Ganapati having named after his father a big agrahāram of great renown on the bank of the river Krishna, gave with pleasure the Agrahāram to the best of the Brahmins who were well-versed in the Vedas, and all the branches of knowledge, and who have specialised in that branch namely, 'Sukla Yajurvēda which has been reputed to be the first among all the branches of the Vēda and who had the honour of having Yāgñavalkya as their progenitor[6]. The Rājaguru Viśveśvara Śiva gave a vṛitti of two puṭṭis of land each to the three teachers of the Rig, Yajur and the Sāmavēdas and to the five expounders of logic, literature and the Āgamas at Viśvēśvara Gōḷaki[7].

Thus these teachers lived a life dedicated to the spread of knowledge. Students who sought the pursuit of such subjects remained in the homes of their teachers to study and both the teachers and the pupil were left to persue knowledge in peace undisturbed by any mundane factors. If at all the king Gaṇapati and his heir Rudrama or Pratāparudra, or his guru of nobles, interfered, it was only to give them maintenance gifts, which would take care of their material needs. Agrahāras verily became the Vidyapitas, the centres of education and culture, during the reign of Gaṇapatidēva.

Yagñas and Yāgas were in vogue. Tikkana was a Sōmayaji, meaning the one who has performed the sacrifice. Viddhanāchārya performed the Sarvatōmukha and Agnishtōma[8] sacrifices.

As a result of their scholarship and of membership of the highest caste, the Brahmins as a class enjoyed certain privileges. One such privilege was exemption from the payment of taxes in several cases. Whenever they were granted Agrahāras, those Agrahāras were given free of taxes[9]. Brahmins who did not belong to Agraharas also enjoyed this privilege. Thus the temple priests of Dengarabudi were exempted from the payment of duties on the sale of houses. Another privilege enjoyed by the Brahmins was the exemption from capital punishment. Mallikārjuna in his *Śivatatvasāra* makes mention of this[10].

To ascertain the position of the Brahmin in the society of the day it is necessary to make a reference to *Vignaneswariyamu* written by the poet Kētana. The work is based on Mitākshara written in the eleventh century by Vignanēśvara. Kētana himself lived in the thirteenth and early part of the fourteenth century. So far as the position of the Brahmins is concerned there are three points which come out prominently in Kētana work. One is the privileged position which the Brahmin occupied in society. The second is the emphasis on the need for maintaining outward distinction between the Brahmins on one hand and the Kshatriyas and Vaiśyas on the other even though all of them were classed as Dvijas. The third is the greater rigidity of the rules which the Brahmin was expected to follow.

There were differences in punishments among various castes. Brahmins had many concessions in punishments. The worst and the most difficult ordeal was imposed on the Sudras. The upanayana was performed by the Brahmins, the Kshatriyas and Vaisya but while the age fixed for the upanayana of a Brahmin was eight, it was eleven for a Kshatriya and twelve for a Vaisya. The stick which a Brahmin was to use during the upanayana ceremony was made of 'Mārēdu' or 'Mōduga'. In the case of a Kshatriya it is 'Vata' and for Vaiśya 'Ravi' or 'Mēdi'.

Though the Brahmin occupied a privileged position, there were more restrictions on his freedom and he had to lead a much more austere life. He had to bath in cold water early in the morning. He had also to bath when he touched a chandāla or a member of communities like Jalagari, Goḍagari, etc. There were more restrictions on the kind of food which he was permitted to eat. He should observe more rules of cleanliness than members of other castes. He had to spend more time every day on religious ceremonies than others.

The above restrictions were not accepted by several people as restrictions. They regarded them only as a disciplined way of life.

Kshatriyas

Next to Brahmins the Kshatriyas occupied an important place in society. They were the ruling caste. According to tradition they fell into two groups, the Solar and Lunar, according to their descent from the Sun or the Moon. They followed the military profession and who do not came across Kshatriyas took to any profession other than fighting and ruling. But it should be noted that all the rulers of the day and all those who took the military service did not belong to the Kshatriya caste. Among the rulers there were several who belonged to the Sūdra caste. Mandalikas for example belonged to the Dūrjaya family of the fourth caste. After they became rulers their status in the social hierarchy was raised and they came to be recognised as Kshatriyas and the rulers who were Kshatriyas by tradition entered into marriage alliance with them. The Kākatīyas of Warangal belonged to the fourth caste but the two daughters Mailāṁba and Kundāṁba of the Kakatiya king

Mahādeva married Nattavāḍi Rudra a Kshatriya chief. Rudrama the daugher of Kākati king Gaṇapati married the Eastern Chāḷukya Vīrabhadra, a Kshatriya.

The large bulk of the army in every kingdom consisted of Sudras. Several of them rose to great eminance by dint of their fighting capacity and valour and were rewarded with Governorship. The Kākatīyas rose to be independent after first securing the position of Governors.

The Vaisyas

The Vaisyas occupied the third place. The Vaisyas are called 'Kōmatis' and 'Settis'[11]. The word 'Komati' seems to have been first used in Literature *Neeti Sāstra Muktāvai* written by Bhadrabhūpala[12]. There is reference to the Dākarēmi Kōmaṭlu in an inscription[13]. Kōmatlu and Seṭṭis are used more or less synonymously. Trade was their main occupation though they had no monopoly over it. Members of other communities like Balijas, Gavaras and Telikas also carried on trade and affixed the terms 'Setty' and 'Kōmaṭi' to their names.

Sūdras

All those among the caste Hindus who did not belong to the Brahmin, Kshatriya and Vaisya castes fell into the category of Sūdras. The Sūdras represented the vast majority of the population. A few records speak of eighteen communities, without giving the full details. Some of the communities were the Kōmaṭis (Traders), Ideras (the toddy tappers), Collavāru (Cowherds), Akkasālavāru (Goldsmiths), Sālevāru (Weavers), Mangalūru (Barbers), Kummaravāru (Potters), etc[14]. The names with suffixes Reḍḍi and Nāyudu found in inscriptions reveal the existence of these communities[15]. The cherakas, rēcherlas, gonas, etc. were termed as Reḍḍis[16]. Reḍḍi was the designation of a person on whom the lordship of a territory was conferred. It is quite possible that the families whose members occupied the position of Reddi for some generations formed the community of Reddis which had played a prominent part in the history of Āndhra from the fourteenth century onwards.

Vallabhamatya's *Kṛiḍabhīrāmamu* and Palkuriki Somanadha's *Basavapurānamu,* give the names of some communities like Kāpu, Telika, Mēdari, Watermen and Chanḍāla[17]. The Telika were oilmongers, the mēdaris wove baskets and mats. The Chanḍālas formed the lowest rung in society. They were the 'antaranivaru', the untouchables. Their proximity was prohibited when religious ceremonies were performed in the agrahāras. The status of these outcastes underwent a change during the Kākatīya age. The *Palanātivīracharitra* speaks of Brahmaṇāyuḍu of Palnāḍu, a contemporary of Rudra-I who initiated interdining and inter-marriages with them[18]. Viśvēśvara Śiva, the spiritual guru of Gaṇapatidēva established a new village with the name of Viśvēśvaradēva and peopled it with persons of different castes from various parts of the country. He established the Gōlaki Maṭha there. There was a choultry attached to it in which all classes of persons from the Brahmins to the Chanḍāla were fed. In the days of Rudradēvi a feeding house was established which fed even these Chanḍālas. It was considered to be pious and meritorious act to provide them with food[19]. Though the Chanḍālas for agriculture as they formed the bulk of agricultural labour. Ēkavīra and village deities were worshipped by them.

The Veera Śaiviṭe teachers preach the spiritual equality of all classes including chanḍālas. According to them if a person is an ardent follower of Veera Śaivism he should be respected even if he was a chandala or untouchable by birth. Srīpati Panḍita dined in the house of a low caste Godagari and he justified his act by saying that 'among the devotees of Siva there is none, high or low, all are one and equal'. From these accounts it could be very well stated that there were tendencies towards liberalism in the treatment of Chanḍālas.

Position of Women

In describing the position and status of women, it may be noted at the outset that in the main it conformed to the dictim laid down by Manu, the great law giver that 'a women does not deserve freedom' and that her life should throughout be one of dependence on man[20]. There was nothing peculiar in this as it was a feature characteristic of all patriarchally organised societies of the world including the west in the pre-industrial age. It was only in some primitive societies which were matriarchial in character that women held a position equal to and some times superior to that of man[21]. In patriarchal society as it developed in India, women was dependent as a girl on her father, as a wife on her husband and as a widow on her son. She did not participate directly in public life and no career or public position was open to her. There were of course a few like the Kākatīya Rudramadēvi who ruled as queen and a few like the Palnāṭi Nāyakurālu who distinguished herself as a Minister. But these were exceptions to the general rule. She had her recognised place in it and especially as mother of children she was for the bringing-up and proper training of children she was held in great esteem. She had unique place in the family as having the same divinitiy in her as the father had.

In the literary works and inscriptions of the period we come across three categories of women—the family women (Kula stree), the courtesan (the Bhoga stree) and the prostitute (the vēsya). Most women belonged to the first category and the other classes formed only a small minority.

Family Women

The family women (kula stree) was the legitimate wife of man. Devotion to her husband was the one duty that was expected of her and this was considered to be the highest womanly virtue. In additon to that, she had her duties to her children as their mother, to look after and manage the household.

She was the ministers of the house (griha-patni). This meant a busy life for her from morning until she went to bed.

In Nannechōḍa's Kumāra Sambhava there is a verse which tells how girls spent their time in making toys of clay, wood and ivory, building of toy-houses, cooking and celebrating toy marriages and worshipping Siva[22]. Women of the higher castes were confines to the house-hold and rarely came out. Even if they came out it was generally in the company of their husbands or other male relatives.

There was some departure from the extreme dependence of women on men in the Vīra Śaiva society, the new society which came into existence as a result of militant Śaivism. Vīra Śaiva teachers declared that women had a right to ignore their husbands if the latter did not believe in Linga worship and in the supremacy of Lord Siva. Mallikarjuna says in his Śivatatvasāramu that if the wife fails in bringing her husband round to her religious beliefs she might abandon him[23].

Both the literary works and inscriptions show that women were held in great esteem. In the inscriptions of the period, the donors made mention not only of their father but also of their mothers in respectable terms. For example an inscription dated S.1142 (1220 A.D.) speaks of Marisetṭi, grandson of Pallakommsetṭi who made a gift of twenty-five cows and one breeding bull for a perpetual lamp in the temple of Jelādhiśwara of Ghanṭaśāla not only in the name of his father but also of his mother Surasāni[24]. The term 'Sani' contrary to the present meaning was used to denote ladies of respectable families of any caste or class. Epigraphical evidence shows that mothers of ruling chiefs, nobles as well as the Brahmin, Vaisya and Sūdra women were called Sanis.

The general dependence of women on men did not stand in the way of women making religious endowments in their own names. We come across women of different castes and of different ranks making endowments either to temples, choultries or other works of public utility and to Brahmins. An inscription, dated S.1131 (1209 A.D.) states that Melaṁbika, a sister of Kākatī Gaṇapatidēva and wife of Ekkadi Mallarudradēva consecreted the image of Mailaṁbikēśwara.[25]

The cōḍes of ancient and medieval writers also contain provision for entertaining women in royal service, industry and agriculture. Jāyapa in his Nṛitta Ratnavāli says that the king while watching a dance perfomance should be attended by women who would fan him and specially by a well talented women to explain to the king the significance of each type of dance.[26]

There were women who were trained to become rulers and were also successful. Rudramadēvi, the eldest daughter of king Gaṇapati during the life time of her father was given training in administration as well as fighting. Rudrama, after the death of her father succeeded to the throne.

Kākati Gaṇapaṁba (younger daughter of Ganapati) though not as famous as Rudrama used to carry on the administration in absence of her husband Beta and assumed on his death in about A.D. 1253 the reigns of the government and ruled the principality for well over forty years as its undisputed ruler.

Courtesans

During this period as in other ages we come across the class of courtesans who usually known as Bhoga streelu distinct from family women. They formed an important community and were attached to courts of kings, to nobles and to temples. They may be said to have corresponded to the Hetaena in Greek society. They were generally not married. They were accomplished in music, dancing and several other fine arts and they were employed as singers, dancers.

To be a courtesan was not considered to be immoral in those days, when polygamy was permitted and practised to some extent by all classes of people. Women of this class occasionally rose to great eminence because of their status as the concubines (the Lanja-pandlamu) of the ruling princes or noblemen.

Quite often we come across the phrase 'Sānulu-Mānulu'. Sānulu seems to mean from the context in which the word occurs, the women employed in temples. They were accomplished in dancing, music and in several other fine arts and they dedicated their lives to the service of Gods in temples. The Sānulu might even have been married and might have children.

Attached to the temples we come across a class of women known as 'Sāni Munnuru'. They belonged to a guild of Sanis.

In the temples of both Siva and Vishṇu we come across a number of Sanis known as Sānulu, Nartaki and Gayaki employed in the temples to sing and dance. They received either gifts of land or cash made by private individuals or regular pay as members of the staff of the temple. They waved fans and also performed other services upachāras to the deity. But there were Sāmpradaya Sānulu who were permanent employees of the temple and whose position was hereditary. There is reference to thirty Sāmpradaya Sanulu attached to Sri Kurmaśwami temple[27]. Next we come across 'Hrita' or one who was presented to a temple.

An inscription of Jāyapa from Chēbrōlu, the chief of Kākati Gaṇapati refers to three hundred dancing girls, who served in the temple from the age of eight years. There was a dancing master also attached to that temple at Chēbrōlu[28]. This shows that the dancing girls were in the service of the temple right from their childhood and they were given training in all fine arts by talented masters.

Vēsyas (Prostitutes)

Frequent references are found to them in literary writings like Sōmanātha's *Paṇḍitarādhya charitra.* They were deservedly not held in esteem in society and were looked at with contempt because of their profession and with fear because they were believed to be conversant in all sorts of tricks to entice men and bring ruin on them and their families.

Sōmanatha gives a detailed description of their manners in his *Paṇḍitarādhya charitra.* He compares them to thieves and robbers and tells their cruelty knows no limits. The vēsyas lived in separate localities in towns. There were references to their beauty and accomplishments in the books of the time and inscriptions. They were even more notorious for their skill in extracting money from the men who resorted to their house.

There are also references to Kunteneelu, women who served as touts or brokers in the service of Vēsyas[29]. Sometimes the Vesya mata herself served as a tout. Along with descriptions Vēsya there are also description of Vēsya matas—the mothers of the Vēsyas. Ōrugallu had its own separate Vēsya vatika where these Vēsyas lived. Rules and regulations determined their professional conduct. There is the story given in *Kreedabhīrāmam* of a stranger belonging to Tunḍirasima coming all the way to Ōrugaḷḷu, the Kākatīya capital and got a Vēsya fixed for him through her mother in return for a certain amount of money but ultimately she deceived him. He then lodged a case before the Judges in the town who ordered the punishment of the Vēśya mata for the crime of cheating a stranger[30].

It may also be that among the Vēśyas there were caste distinctions or regional distinctions. In *Kṛeeḍabhīramamu* there is a reference to a Karnataka Vēśya, to a Medara Karana Vēśya and to a Ganula Karana who belonged to the caste of oilpressers[31]. The Vēśyas were very particular about their dress and there was much demand from them for tailors[32].

Occupation of Women

The occupation of women who were skilled in some occupations and who earned money out of them.

(a) Mēdaras of Basket markets were one such class. Their profession was known as 'Katākara vṛitti'.[33] They were specially skilled in weaving mats and in making baskets and other articles of bamboo.

(b) 'Pushpalavikulu' and 'Malakarulu'[34] the women who were skilled in making flower garlands. They made money from the regular sale of flowers and flower garlands. Some of them were attached to temples.

(c) Telika women or oil-pressers[35]. They engaged themselves not only in pressing oil but also in the making and sale of 'Sampangi-nūone' a kind of perfume oil. Several women maintained inns and hotels known as 'Pūtakuḷḷa Iḷḷu'[36] the usual charge for meal being one Ruka. Several classes of women took to fruitful occupations.

Though certain classes of women especially those who belonged to the ruling aristrocracy used some kind of veil (Mēli-musugu) there was no strict use of Purdah. There are several references in contemporary literature to women moving freely and publicly in the presence of men.

The women so far referred to were those who belonged to the general mass of the population and who lived in villages and towns. But there were women belonged to the various forest tribes—the Erukulas, the Sabaras, etc. The Erukulas were tribes of nomads and the Erukula women are described as having special skill in palmistry. Their services were in great demand. The Sabara women lived in forests and were specially known for their knowledge of the habits of animals after which they wandered. They were also known for their bravery and courage. They enjoyed complete freedom and did not submit themselves to men.

The Education of Women

When there was no systematic education for the men, there in no wonder that women were not imparted any formal education. At that time the existing categories of women learning formal education were—royal families or women of aristocratic families and the women of the class—courtesans and prostitutes.

Vātsyayana in his *Kāmasāstra* states that, besides reading, writing and arithmetic the following subjects are essential for them in the curriculum of studies. The subjects to be learnt by the women are :

1. Singing, dancing and playing on musical instruments.
2. Drawing.
3. Hand-work.
   (a) Arranging idols, adorning idols with rice and flowers.
   (b) Drawing figures with flowers on the ground, arranging beds and couches with flowers, etc.
   (c) Colouring teeth, garments, hair, nails and bodies.
   (d) Making figures and images.
   (e) Cooking and making drinks
   (f) Disposition of Jewels and decoration and dress
4. Speech training.
5. General knowledge.
6. Subjects of recreation, solution of riddles, verbal puzzels, etc.
7. Physical training—Phyical exercise with sword, stick, quarter staff, bow and arrow.

Only women who had sufficient leisure were in a position to study several subjects. From the literature of the medieval period we learn that women of royal families received education in the subjects listed above. We have several instances of women proficient in the above subjects.

Girls of royal family were also training in the art of fighting and in statecraft. For instance Gaṇapati trained his daughters Rudrama and Gaṇapāṁba in the art of fighting and in statecraft.

Women of comman classes did not receive formal education of the type mentioned above. But they were all interested in listening to puranas and epics specially when they were recited in temples on certain occasions like Sivaratri.

The education of the courtesan varied in some respects from that of the members of the higher castes. Without exception in those days every dancing girl was given training in literature, dancing, music and other fine arts.

Women and Marriages

Marriages is the most important Samskara. It is a holy act, according to the Sastras to be performed by the Hindus. It is very important because of the full scope of the relationship of first three ends of man namely pleasure (Kāma), material gain (Artha) and Virtue (Dharma).

Marriages in those days were arranged by parents and elders. Sometimes marriages among the ruling classes were arranged by parents on political grounds. Regarding the age of marriage, boys and girls were usually married quite young though there were exceptions in the case of princesses. It was customary among all classes of people to give dowry to the daughter at the time of her marriage. It was known as 'Arnamu'. It was merely the gift given by the father at the time of the marriage of his daughter or after the marriage.

Polygamy seem to have been quite common among members of the royal family. In addition to her own mother Sōmaṁba, Rudradēvi had two step-mothers, Nāraṁba and Pēraṁba.

Society did not propagate the glories of the burning of widows along with their dead husbands. Widows lived to lead an active and useful life as administrators, temple builders and benefactors, though they never married again. The kingdom was ruled by Rudrama, whose consort had departed earlier. Her sister Gaṇapāṁba administered for her late husband Kota Beta[37], and spent her time building temples.

Common ladies too could enjoy the grants of land and gardens, gifted to their dead husbands, even in the absence of sons. The Malkapuram grant makes a provision for such a contingency. Such ladies could enjoy their grants taking the help of others in their work[38]. Evidently the life of a widow was not made intolerable for her to see redemption in Sahagamana.

As no society, however, progressive is entirely free of superstitions, Gaṇapati and his people too had their own beliefs in omens and astrologers, who foretold future events. An auspicious movement or such muhurtam was considerd highly effective to start any work, whether for commencing agricultural operations or setting out an expeditions of conquest. This necessitated the measuring of time and announcing it to the public. The device that helped this purpose called 'Gadiyaramu' was popularised under Kākatīyas. *Kṛiḍahīrāmamu* refers to a Gadiyaramu which was kept in the entrance hall (Mosala) of the Kākatīya royal palace. Hearing the Gadiyaramu strike sixteen gadiyas, Mancana Sarma and Tittibha seṭṭi then visiting Ekasilanagara decided to go to the Puṭakuṭiḷḷu for lunch. Such hotels also served as rendzvous for clandestine meetings.[39]

Peculiar Customs and Rites

'Saivism by nature was a martial religion' and it became more so in the medieval age. The Tantric cult of Saivism which entered the Telinga country during the medieval period popularised certain rites which were until then, rare and unpopular[40]. One such rite was self-immolation. Devotees in their excessive zeal cut out their own heads or mutilated themselves to propitiate their Gods. This practice was in evidence in South India, as early as the *Silāppādīkāram,* the Tamil classic. The tantric cult of the medieval period and the Pāsupata Saivism which reigned supreme in the Kākatīya land gave this custom a fresh impetus. For members of the Saiva communities, like Vīrabhadras, Viramushṭis and Mailara Vīrabhadras, such self infliction became a part and parcel of their lives[41]. They gave up their gladly or mutilated themselves for a noble cause or ideal, for the welfare of the community, or in their exessive devotion to their God. The Mailara Vīrabhadras mutilated themselves in fulfilment of their vows. The Vīrabhadras and Vīramushṭis gave up their lives for a cause or in protecting the people. Even young girls sacrificed themselves for the safety of their village. Such self-sacrifice for a cause received great commendation from the society and the martyr naturally became a hero and a saint. They were honoured and remembered in their sculpture forms, the Virakals. Saivite centres like Tripurāntakaṁ, Nopuru, Kārempudi, Macherla and Warangal redound in these Virakals or herostones.[42]

At Tripurantakam there are numerous such Virakals representing "human figures in various postures, some with a dagger thrust into their neck or abdomen, left thigh, chest, etc. One peculiar feature of these figure is the long braided hair which is gracefully allowed to hang right upto the knee."[43]

Gradually these hero-stones acquired such a sanctity that a 'Vira chara', the cult of heros developed towards the end of Kākatīya rule.

Food

The food habits of the Andhras are mentioned in a few sources. The Siddēśavara Charitra mentions modakalu (sweet-meals) and Panakamu (fruit juice) which the Puṭakuṭillu served. Dishes made with wheat, vegetables curries and butter-milk, pickles were great favourites. In the heart of the city in the mad santa (market fair) grains and vegetables were sold and flesh was sold outside the city in market fair called the mailla santa.[44] Marcopolo observed that 'they live on rice, flesh milk, fish and fruit.'[45]

Mangoes, bananas, maduphala, kammarenu, etc. were some of the fruits liked by the people. Arecanuts and coconuts were used. Rice, wheat, green lentils, cholam, ginger, mustard, pepper, honey, turmeric, kanugh oil, gingelly oil, ghee, etc. are mentioned in records of the period.

Dress

There is meagre information about the apparel of the people. Sari (chira) is the most important in the dress of women, coming from time immemorial. The women of the period under review wore sarees made of ordinary cloth, fine cloth, and silk. The bodice (ravika) and jacket (kuppasamu) were worn by women along with saries. They were lightly tied round the body and on neck, making the Mangalasutra clearly visible. They had a wide range of choice in different colours and designs. While there were the tailors (kutrapuvandru) to stitch clothes, there were another category, the Maharivandlu, specialised in stitching battle array.[45] Shoes were used by women when they went to other places, especially during the pilgrimage.

Men wore two pieces of cloth one below the waist and the other, about it, called dovati and uttariyam respectively. While the commoners wore cotton cloths, rich people preferred silks and brocades like the dasuri-paṭṭu, pachcha-paṭṭu, chinambaramu, etc. Cotton and silk were woven at Orugallu itself, while the Chīnāmbaram was imported from China[46].

Ornaments

Without an intimate knowledge of customs and manners of the times, it is impossible to get at their true meaning as many of the ornaments have fallen into dis-use owing to social conditions affected by political trends.

Ornaments were worn by women from head to foot and the metals used also varied according to their status in society. Whatever may be the metal of ornaments, the Mangala sutra, the emblem of the married women was invariably made of gold. Generally all the ornaments were made of gold but yōgins and persons belonging to hill tribes, used ornaments of brass and iron.

Both men and women loved to deck themselves with jewellery. Kridabhiramamu speaks of a variety of bracelets and bangles, rings, ear-rings and necklaces of gold studded with jems, like diamonds, pearls, corals, etc. Married ladies alone wore toe-rings called mattulu.[48]

People high and low had to protect themselves from severe summer sun. Sandals and umbrellas were a necessity. In the Telugu country a particular type of sandalas made a creaking sound and hence were called 'kirru cheppulu'. There were many types of umbrellas. Those made of palm leaves sheltered the ordinary while those made of silk and costlier material served the aristocrates. Moreover the umbrella was a sign of honour and status.

Perfumes

Perumes lent an air of fragrance and men and women could never resist perfumeries like sandal, camphor, rose-water, musk (kasturi), etc. Long tussels found favour in contemporary fashions. Those not thus gifted made it up with false hair (savaralu). Hair was dressed either in braids or pulled up in attractive coiffures. They chewed betel-leaves to lighten the colour of their lips.

Ammusements

People amused themselves variously. The astounding feats of the Mailanra Vīrabhadras who walked on fire, jumped into iron spikes, swallowed iron labis, etc. held their attention. Dice, cook-fights, the snake charmer and such other sports formed great attractions for the people. Girls amused themselves playing with ball, music and dance. Painting and such other fine arts attracted the more refined.[49] Musicians and dancers were patronised by the royalty and the aristrocracy,[50] and there were a variety of instruments too. There were the Mrudanga or maddela (a small drum), randhrapuraka, kahala (a trumpet), karada, etc.[51]

During the reign of Ganapatideva, generally speaking there was contentment and prosperity in society. People led a life rich and colourful under the fostering care of Ganapatidēva.

References

1. M. Somasekhara Sarma–*History of the Reddi Kingdoms*, p. 256.
2. *Sid. Cha.*, pp. 115-16.
3. *S.I.I.*, Vol. X, No. 395, Vs. 68 to 70.
4. *S.I.I.*, Vol. X, No. 395; *C.T.I.*, II, No. 52; *A.R.E.* 19 of 1961-62.
5. *S.I.I.*, Vol. X, No.151.
6. *J.A.H.R.S.*, Vol. 1, Part II.
7. *S.I.I.*, Vol. X, No. 395.
8. *Sid. Cha.*; *A.R.E.* 19 of 1961-62.
9. *S.I.I.*, Vol. X, Nos. 119, 248, etc.
10. Mallikarjuna's *Sivatatvasaramu*, Vol. 213.
11. *S.I.I.*, Vol. X, No. 373.
12. Komati Paduchu Nolla–*Neeti Sastra*, Ist verse.
13. *S.I.I.*, Vol. X, No. 114.
14. *C.T.I.*, II, No. 30, Nagulapadu Inscription; No. 26 Mellacheruvu inscription.
15. *S.I.I.*, Vol. X, Nos. 460, 473, 476; *C.T.I.*, II, No. 261; *S.I.I.*, Vol. X, Nos. 442, 471 and 472.
16. *A.R.E.* 321, 322 of 1937; *S.I.I.*, Vol. X, No. 473, 460 and 476.
17. *Kridabhiramamu* and *Basavapuranamu*–a long list of communities are mentioned in the *Pratapacharitra* and the *Siddhesvara charitra.*
18. *Palnativira Charitra* by Srinadha–Palanadu is the present Palnad of

the Guntur district.

19. "Kadejavani Yakali dirchina yatandu Karmarth Svarga likamuna nundu"—*Rukmangada Charitra* by Praudhakavi Mallana, II, Vol. 77.
20. Manu III, Ch. 7, p. 55.
21. R.M. MacIver, *Society*, p. 248.
22. Nanne Choda's *Kumarasambhava*, Canto III, verse 37.
23. Mallikarjuna's *Sivatatvasaramu*, verse 231.
24. *S.I.I.*, Vol. X, No. 82.
25. *Ibid.*, No. 254.
26. Jayapa, *Nritta Ratnavali*, Ch. VIII, Bhavaprakasika unpublished.
27. *A.R.E*, 1925, No. 564.
28. *E.I.*, Vol. V, dated 1898-99; Chebrolu inscription of Jayapa.
29. Ketana's *Dasakumara Charitra*, Canto V, Verse 49.
30. Vallabaraya's *Kreedabhiramamu*, Verses 36 to 38.
31. *Ibid.*, Verses 101-5.
32. *Ibid.*, Verses 106
33. *Ibid.*, Verses 67
34. *Ibid.*, Verses 174
35. Vallabharaya's *Kreedabhiramamu*, Verses 103.
36. *Ibid.*, Verses 158-60.
37. *S.I.I.*, Vol. X, No. 381.
38. *A.R.E.*, 94 of 1917, The Malkapuram inscription, Vols. 66-67.
39. *Kreedabhiramamu*
40. *History of the Reddi Kingdoms*, p. 339.
41. A.P. Govt. Arch. Series, No. 15—The Archaeological Bulletin No. II.
42. Tripurantakam, Nopuru, Karempudi and Macherala and Warangal are in the present Kurnool, Cuddapah, Guntur and Warangal districts respectively.
43. A.P. Govt. Arch. Series, No. 15—The Archaeological Bulleitin No. II, Section III–Museums. A note on medieval sculpture in Hyderabad Museum depicting self-immolation. There are also different hair styles in the form of a loop and not left hanging down the back.
44. *Kr. Ra.*

45. Travels of Marcopolo translated by A. Riccu.
46. *Kr. Ra.*; The *Sid. Cha.* mentions Maravandlu (dress makers) and the *Kr. Ra.* refers to the mohari-wada a locality where the moharivandlu stitched battle uniform, according to Sri V. Prabhakara Sastry, the Editor of *Kr. Ra.*
47. *C.T.I.* II, No. 14; *Sid. Cha.* Introduction, p. 77; *History of Reddi Kingdoms*, p. 408.
48. (a) *Kr. Ra.*

    (b) Travels of Marcopolo.

    (c) *C.T.I.* Part II, No. 14, Warangal.
49. *Kr. Ra.*, Vol. 142.
50. *A.R.E.* of 94 of 1917; *C.T.I.*, II, No. 1.
51. *Sivavogasaramu* gives names of more musical instruments.

6

Economic Conditions

Very little is known about the economic condition of the people of Kākatīya kingdom during the reign of Gaṇapatidēva. Sources are meagre and it is easy to give a clear and detailed picture of the economic condition of a bygone age in India. Only the broad outlines can be attempted at.

Agriculture

The Kākatīyas realised the need for the improvement of economic resources of the empire and paid much attention to agriculture, for it was the primary source of revenue. This policy was pursued in three directions, viz., 1. Construcion of a large network of tanks, 2. Reclamation of deserted villages and lands and 3. Formation of new villages and granting them as agrahāras to brahmins. The Kākatīya kingdom contained red and sandy soil. Though very fertile, it mainly depended upon rain water, except in valleys and deltas of rivers like the Krishṇa, the Gōdavari the Tungabhadra and the Pennar. The character of Telangāṇa soil required plentiful supply of water. The land was highly suitable for wet cultivation.

The construction of tank was regarded as an act of charity resulting in the acquisition of great religious merit. It was regarded as one of the seven meritorious acts. Saptasantānas include the following. One's own son, Adopted son, Literary work, an Agrahāra, a garden, a tank, a temple[1].

The sporadic allusions in inscriptions and literary compositions to the construction of tanks and dykes that are scattered and the numerous remains of the old irrigational works that are distributed in the Telanagāṇa region of Andhra Pradesh bear testimony to the care with which such facilities were provided by the Kākatiya kings. The Mōṭupalli pillar inscriptions of Gaṇapatidēva records that Prōla-II excavated a tank known as Kēsari-taṭakam which was like 'a representative of the ocean and the collection of all waters that were originally created'[2]. Bēta-II laid out a garden and tank named Śivapura in the city of Hanumankonḍa[3]. He is said to have undertaken the building of two tanks namely Seṭṭi Kereya and Kēsari Samudra and to have performed in that connection the ceremony of Veruṇa Pratishṭa or the installation of Varuṇa, the presiding deity of waters[4]. The Pratāpa Charitra mentions the Gaṇapatidēva founded many tanks at Nellore, Gangāpuram, Ellore, Gaṇapapuram Ēkaśilapuri, etc[5]. The same authority credits Rudramadēvi and Pratāparudradēva with the construction of many tanks[6].

The Kākatīya kings as well as the nobles and officials like other over-lords also took interest in the construction of tanks. But the kings as heads of the state did not take any direct reponsibility for providing such facilities. The records of Kākatīya rulers did not mention any public works department with the task of irrigation[7]. The Konḍiparti epigraph dated Śaka 1125 records that during the reign of Gaṇapatidēva the general Chaunḍa of the Malyāla family constructed an extensive tank which belw away the pride of all oceans and named it as Chaunḍa-Samudra[8]. The Upparapalli epigraph dated in Saka 1157 (A.D.1235) refers to various canals which constituted a part of the boundaries of lands which Kaṭaya, who was in the service of Gaṇapatidēva, gifted to the five lingas[9]. The Sōmavaram inscription dated A.D. 1213 records that Rēcherla Beti Reḍḍi established two tanks[10]. Annaya of the Indulūri family is said to have constructed many tanks along with the banks to be the ocean and his consorts respectively[11]

The Hanumakonda Nirōshtya-Kāvya inscription states 'in the country (i.e., Āndhradēsa) are hundreds of tanks and thousands of riverlets and they indeed appear to be the ocean and his consorts respectively[12].

A large number of tanks with suffixes, Samudra, Cheṛuvu or Teṛuvu and Kere or Kēreya are referred to in the inscriptions. Samudra may be a tank having large dimensions and supplying water for some thousands of acres. Cheṛuvu may be a village tank where as Kereya may be Kanada equivalent for a village tank. Some of them are as follows :

Samudras :

Kēsari Samudra[3]
Prōla Samudra[14]
Udaya Samudra[15]
Gaṇapa Samudra[16]
Chaunḍa Samudra[17]

Cheṛuvus or Teṛuvus :

Manḍaraju Cheṛuvu[18]
Cuṁtala Cheṛuvu[19]
Guḍla Cheṛuvu[20]
Sōmiseṭṭi Cheṛuvu[21]
Kolikudla Cheṛuvu[22]

Kereya :

The Hanumakonḍa inscription of Betena mentions a tank known as setti-kereya.[23]

It is evident from the above discussion that the Cheṛuvus or teṛuvus or Kereyas were named after the persons who excavated them or the donor or the name of the person for whose merit it was built or the villages where they were located. The suffixes Samudra, Cheṛuvu of Kereya were attached to them. It would be of absorting interest to mention in this connection that some of the irrigational works founded by Kākatīyas are in existence and irrigating some thousands of areas in the Telangāṇa region of Andhra Pradesh even today. Dr. Gulam Yazdani observes. "Warangal, the metropolitus of this dynasty abounds in magnificient tanks, and the titanic dykes and sluice gates of Pākhal, Lakhmavaram and Rāmappa lakes are object lessons even to the modern engineer."[24]

Pākhal Lake

It is situated about 32 miles east of Waragal and 9 miles away from Necconḍa Railway station and 7 miles north-east of Narasampet, the taluk headquarters. The lake lies in the basins of the Kṛishṇa and the Mamair rivers. The combined drainage area of the lake is 80 sq. miles of which 40 sq. miles are intercepted. The annual rainfall in the basin is 40 and the yield from the catchment amounts to 2987 Mc. feet. The capacity of the tank is 2452 Mc. ft. capable of irrigating about 17258 acres. The lake is not known to have dried up and there are crocodiles in it.[25] According to a pillar inscription which is standing in the centre of the bund, it was constructed during the time of Gaṇapatidēva mahārāja.[15]

Rāmappa Lake

It is situated at a distance of 44 miles north-east of Warangal and 12 miles from Mulug, the headquarters of the same taluka. The epigraphic evidence shows that it was also constructed during the reign of Gaṇapatidēva.[27]

Ghanpūr Lake

It is situated nearly 6 miles away from the Rāmappa lake. Tradition attributes the credit of constructing this tank to Gaṇapatidēva.

Besides the above mentioned lakes and tanks there were many other tanks which are in very good condition today. They are—Udaya Samudra (near Pānugal in the Nalgonḍa district) Malla Samudram (near Matedu in the Khammam district), and the Bayyaram Ceruvu (near Bayyāram in the same district).[28]

The maintenance of irrigation works was atleast as important as the construction of new ones. Their maintenance involved the repair of damaged tanks and the removal of silt in order to prevent the tank or other irrigation work from being closed up. Generally the state, the village community and the private individuals appear to have taken keen interest in these matters.

Closely connected with the tanks and lakes is the excavation of Kāluvus (canals) and tumus (sluices). An inscription refers to the construction of a canal by Malyala Gunda.[29]

The canals were dug to bring water from the rivers to fill the tanks situated in the vicinity. Of this class may be mentioned the Museti-Kaluva, Antaranga Kāluva, Kṛishnavēni Kāluva. etc.[30] They were also dug to carry water from the tanks to water the fields. Sub-soil water from springs and Uta-Kāluvas was used to fill the tanks in certain areas.[31] In this connection it may be of interest to mention some of the canals that are referred to in the inscriptions during the period under our study. They are as follows :

Tūmu-Kāluva[32]
Tamti-Kāluva[33]
Utum-Kāluva[34]
Medaviroupam-Kāluva[35]
Immagati-Kāluva[36]

Construction of wells and irrigation with the help of well water were known is the Kākatīya period. An inscription dated Saka 1162, records the construction of a well by Malyāla Kāta.[37] Under well-water irrigation, the water drawing mechanism, etam, was used to lift water from wells, either by the use of bullock-power or man-power, to supply water to the fields situated nearby. The Dosapadu inscription, dated 1254 A.D. records the gift of a water-lifting pulley, ratnam, together with two bullocks.[38]

Hired labour, who were paid in cash built the Kumara Samudramu and the Tripura-Samudras. A record of 1294 A.D. from Tripurāntakam gives the amount of expenditure involved in building the above three tanks. Tripura Samudram cost, one hundred fifty-six madas; the Kumara-Samudram cost two hundred and forty one madas.[39] There is no information to say whether this was the only method employed or whether it was just one among the many.

Reclamation from the economic point of view, may be considered as supplying a means of coping with the pressure of population. It was followed in two ways:

1. Clearance of waste or land covered with jungle and bringing it under cultivation for the first time, and
2. Foundation of new villages.

Traditional and archaeological evidence shows that both these types of land reclamation were used in the period under study. The local tradition preserved in the Kaifiyats of several to the West of the Srisaila mountain corresponding to a large portion of the present Nandikotkur taluk of the Kurnool district was also at that time covered by dense woods. The Tripurāntakam inscription of Saka1174-75,[40] refer to the clearance of forests and the construction of tanks.

In granting agraharas and founding new villages the motive might have been acquisition of religious merit for the donor, but there is no doubt that they fulfilled a real economic purpose for a new settlement invariably meant increase of cultivable area by the conversion of the forest tracts into fields.[41] An inscription dated A.D. 1214, records the establishment of a village name Gaṇapatipura.[42] The *Pratāpacharitra* states that Ganapatideva established a village known as Gaṇpatipuram[43]. References to the grants of waste-land, though rare, are not unknown in the inscription of our period. A record from the Nellore district mentions a grant of 1000 Kuntas of dry-waste land to a priest[28]. But the information regarding the concessions that were granted by the state to bring such forests, deserts and waste lands under cultivation is scanty in the extreme. When jungle lands had to be brought under plough, the jungle had to be cleared, stumps had to be excavated and water canals had to be provided. The inducements offered by the state in this connection were assignment of taxes and exemption from taxation. Moreoften, a graduated scale of assessment was adopted to encourage the ryots to bring land under tillage.

Now we may proceed to analyse the material available as regards the agricultural and horticultural products of the time. But an account of agricultural products should begin with the classification of land.

Arable land may be divided broadly into three kinds, viz., Niru-nela (wet land), Veli-polamu (dry land) and Tomta-Polamu (garden land)[44]. The wet land was the most valuable one as it is now, from the economic point of view, for different varieties of paddy were cultivated on it on account of the abundance of water facilities. This was not the case with dry-land. The garden lands were generally located within the village and mainly produced horticultural products.

Fields had a variety of names, and they afford interesting side-lights on the produce of villages. The fields were named after the nature of the soil, its adoptability to particular crop, owenership, and after the name of village, etc. Some of them are given as follows :

1. Kṛishṇa-Ksetra[45]—black-soil, suited for cotton
2. Uppu-bhūmi[46]—or chavuta-bhumi[47]-salty soil
3. Mettu-nela[48]—rocky soil
4. Rēgaḍu[49]—suited for rice
5. Rācha Polamu[50]—crown land
6. Nandigāma polamu[51]—land belonging to the village of Nandigāma

The other varieties of land that are referred to in the epigraphs are griha-ksētra[52] (land suitable for the building of houses), vramta chēnu[53], Kaṁchi-polamu[54], (pasture land), Gosa chēnu[55], Telkula-chēnu[56], Divga chēnu[57], (temple land), Fistala chēnu[58] (land assigned for pay), uttarapu polamu[59] (land situated on the North), etc.

Regarding the size of the fields we have not much evidence. The inscription generally refer to plot of land in terms of marulurus, nivartanas, khandugas, etc. which would indicate the existence of fragmantation of holdings. The occurence of the term achhukattu[60], and adapagattu[61] also indicates the use of balks of unploughed turf making of the various small strips into which the wet-land was divided for purposes of proper irrigation.

Inscriptions give valuable information regarding agricultural and horticultural products of the time. Paddy was the staple crop as is even now. Referring to the rice fields in the village of Gaṇapatipura, the Gaṇapavaram inscription of Śaka 1135 makes the following a large sea like excellent tank, whose water (was) clear and sweet, the paddy crops bent by with the big weight of the ripe corn, drank. This water by the roots which were surrounded by channals and appeared to have bent their heads as if to drink again with their mouths also[62]. The *Bhīmeśavarapurana* says that the Godavari delta region was famous for yielding prasangu type of rice[63].

Wheat (seamum indicum), green lintels, mustard (saladora persica), indigo, maize (Indian corn), castor (recinus communis), tolam, etc. are the other agricultural products mentioned in the inscriptions[64]. Among garden crops, areca-nut (areca-catechu), betal (piper betle), tamarind (tamarindus indica), mangoes (magifera indica), palmyra (borassus flabelliger), citron and sugar-cane figure prominently[65]. The root products like turmeric ginger (zingiber officianle), kanda (typhonium orizfense), etc. and vegetables like potla-kakara (Trichosantties coluorina), Gummadi (cucurbuta pepo), Nirulli (alliumcega), chirugada-dumpa, etc. are also referred to in the inscriptions and literature[66].

The epigraphical evidence gives us some valuable information regarding the system of cultivation that was in vogue during this period. Rotation of crops, double and single, was known. According to the former system, there was one harvest in the month of Karthika in winter and another in the month of Vaisakha in the summer. Under the single crop system there was only one harvest in either of these months. It is recorded that Rēcherla Nāmi Reḍḍi gave some lands to God Namēsvara for cultivation during both the seasons[67].

It is evident from what has been stated above that the Kākatīya kings and their Sāmantas and Mahā-sāmantas paid very keen interest and attention to improving the agricultural potentialities of the empire by excavating tanks, wells and canals, establishing agrahāra villages and bringing under plough the cultivable waste-land.

Taxes

Very little is known about the incidence of taxation during Kākatīya period though the names of many taxes were mentioned in inscription of that period. The main source of revenue for government was taxation on agricultural land. Next to it in value came charges levied on trade and industry. Last but not the least were the assessments of forests and pasture lands on their yields of timber and the value of grazing rights. Taxes were collected by regular officials (both from the sources of income mentioned above and from a number of others). Some of these taxes were conventional and customary and had been in existence from a long time before the appearance of the Kākatīya dynasty. Darisanamu, appanamu and upa-kṛiti were such traditional and accepted charges[53]. Of them the first had to be paid to the king when visiting him on important occasions such as festivals and state ceremonials. This custom of offering presents to the king in kind or in cash at the time of darsan (seeing him) and of paying him kanikas in money on stated occasions remained in vogue till very recent times. Upakriti was another offering consecrated by long usage, paid not only to the king but also to the officials of the state. Gifts thus offered in acknowledgement of some benevolent action on the part of the ruler were known as upakriti. They may be regarded as a kind of customary tax levied by the government on the villagers or townsmen in return for some kind of service permanent of temporary, performed for them.

Kākatīyas provided irrigational facilities which was helped cultivation and extensive land came under the plough. Such cultivable land was categorised differently as nīru-nela (wet land), veli-volamu, veli-chēnu or veli-bhūmi (dry land) and tanta-bhūmi or tonta-polamu (garden-land). The rates of assessment depended on the irrigational facilities provided. Arable land, thus classified, was surveyed by means of a bomboo pole called a gada or damadaka or kola. According to the text books or ganita current in the times of Prataparudra, there were different kinds of poles of varying measurement in use, in different regions and localities. The land measured with a single pole, lengthwise and breadthwise was one henta in extent[69]. House sites were measured by a pole eight 'muras' in length, and fields by a pole twenty four 'muras' in length[70]. According to text books on ganita, the Kesaripati gada was the standard pole in vogue during the time of Prataparudra and probably was not unknown in the reign of Gaṇapatidēva and Rudramadēvi.

The angula, which was half the circumference of the thumb, the length of three yave seeds or half the length of the middle finger, was the unit. Twelve angulas made one Jena and thirty-two jenas one gada or pole[71]. Generally the thumb of a person approved by the king or others chief officers of state is taken for setting the standard unit of angula. Then the pole was measured in accordance with it, and at times a portion of its length was scored on the pillar of a temple for the guidance of future generations. The inscription at Penumuli contains the actual length of the cubits in double line.[72]

Epigraphs reveal some other measuring rods, like the 'Penumbaka mana danda' which was prevalent in and around Penumbaka and the Pedda gada and mentioned in the Mellacheruvu inscription of 1312 A.D.[73]

Both wet and dry lands were measured differently in 'marturu' and 'Khanduka' respectively, with their sub-divisions. Marturu is the plural of 'martu'. The latter became 'Mattar' in the Kannada language. 'Martu' corresponded to a 'nivartana'[74]. The Nivartana had its subdivisions in 'hastas' and 'dandas'. Ten hastas made a danda and thirty dandas made a nivartana. Ten such nivartanas made on gōchama[75].

There was another sub-division called 'adda'[76]. The extent of dry land was measured in Khanḍuva, Khanḍuka or Puṭṭi. The crown lands were called rachapolamu or rachadoddi. Fallow land, which was newly brought under cultivation, was called Chelaka or Cheluka bhūmi and was to be taxed progressively the land being left free during the first three or four years.[77]

Taxes were collected both in cash and in kind. Some of the rates were one chinnamu per marturu of sowable ploughed field; and one chinnamu per putti of dry land[78]. The tax on dry land and garden land was always paid in cash and was respectively known as puṭṭi-palindi and tomta sunkamu.

The royal officers, kolakandru, went round the villages to measure and collect the monarch's share of grain, twice a year, in the months of Kartika (October-November) and

Vaisakha (April-May). They were accompanied by the Tirparulu, who acted as the umpires or judges and saw that no injustice was done either to the cultivator or to the government[79]. A nominal tax on lands gifted to Gods and brahmins, on wet and dry lands, called para and pangamu respectively[80], was collected except on those explicity mentioned above as tax-free. Land tax was generally known as 'ari' and those who paid it were known as 'arigapulu'.

'Suṅkam is a term of broad import'.[81] Inscriptions use it to denote taxes on garden-lands, export and import duties, customs duties on articles of merchandise, excise duties, etc. The task of collecting these were farmed out to merchant guilds or associations comprising members of the trading community like the Ayyavali guild of merchants or Vīrabalanja samaya, on payment of a fixed sum to the government. The procedure adopted in farming out tax-collection and its tenure was unknown. These tax farmers kept several establishments with their distinct official paraphernalia in different places. The guilds enjoyed much freedom and vast powers[82]. The tax collectors were known as Sunkarlu and their accountants, Sunka Karnalu[83]. The money they collected was at times gifted to temples as grants; and inscription registering such grants mentioned in particular articles the duties on which went to the temples. In 1292 A.D. several merchants at Tripurāntakam offered a grant to Lord Tripurāntakadēva of the duties on rice, green gram and ginger in the market of Tripurāntakam.[84]

The unit of measurement and the basis of calculating the duties varied according to the articles. According to a record from Warangal[85] the bandi (cart load) was the unit of measurement for most of the commodities like grain, fruits, oil, ghee, vegetables, coconuts, pickles, ete. Each had to pay quarter for a cart load. In the case of salt, unhusked grain, etc. Peruka was the unit and duties levied were one mana for ten perukas; for betel-leaves it was one 'kavala' (a pack) for a peruka. For sandal-wood and metals like tin, lead, copper, etc. The unit was the 'tulu' (weight) and a 'palam' had to be paid for every tula-javaḍi. Madder, etc. were measured by Mada, 'kode' for ivory and silks; 'malaga' for yarn and cotton piece-goods such as sheets, etc. Other units of measurement, of weight and of value such as mana, annamu or ginnamu, visa, palavina, etc. are referred to. Duty on camphor was two Ṡinnas (annamu?) for a visa; on Javadi, a peruka for a māḍa, on musk two sinnas for a hundred vinas; on silk yarn a cinna for a tula; on maddar, half a visa for a mada; on ivory, dasuri silk and yellow silk, a quarter for a Kode; on coral, a cinna for a visa; on pearls, rosaries, glass-beads and all other stores of precious stones, a visamu for a māda; and on cotton yarn, a quarter for a malama. The whole city of Warangal paid a quarter of rice from each house for the maintenance of the clock called the 'gadiyaramu' and the nakharamu of fair (Santa) paid a buredu (a measurement) of pounded rice per day from every shop for refreshments.

There were a variety of Suṅkams as gathered from records. The 'ammubadi suṅkamu' or 'ammu-kada suṅkam' was the duty payable on sales.

In some inscriptions we come across a tax called peru sumkamu. Perika means a load, especially a load carried on bullocks and 'Peru' seems an alternative form of Perika. Articles of merchandise were used to be carried on the backs of bullocks and other animals and peru sunka seems to have meant a tax levied, on such loads. There was also a tax levied on the sale and purchase of cattle. An inscription dated A.D. 1245 of the time of Kākati Gaṇapatideva states that his agent Pōchana Preggaḍa Gaṇapaya remitted customs duties payable on three hundred bullocks used in importing goods into the town of Tripurāntakam[86].

There was also tax on oil mills. This tax was known as Ganuvula Suṅkamu or Ganuvula Mudra-Suṅkamu. An inscription dated 1247 refers to it[87]. The 'addavatta suṅkamu' was another tax that was prevalent in those days[88]. There appears to have been professional tax, as evidenced by the records. The merchants (Komatis), the Weavers, the Shepherds, the goldsmiths and the toddy-sellers, were obliged to pay a tax[89]. And people who possessed carriages, slaves and horses also paid taxes[90].

Another tax was the tax on marriages. An inscription dated A.D. 1247 from Velpuru refers to a tax on marriages which was assigned to the temple of Rāmēśvara.[91]

Coastal towns like Pedda Ganjamu, Pinaganjamu, Kada-Kulura Chomparela, Keruparli, Devaramupalli, Pandorti, etc. produced salt. The salt pans were managed at times by the merchants and at times by government officials, specially sent, like the 'uppu-suṅkamu-tisedi karanalu'[92]. There were kolakandru to measure salt, and turparalu to sit in judgement.

Land yielded more than one tax. In addition to Ari, there was another unexplained tax called appanamu, Pullari was a grazing tax. Villagers had to pay pullari to let their cattle graze on the government owned pastures and forest lands[93]. There were the various sources of income for the government of Gaṇapatidēva.

The foregoing discussion makes it clear that all classes of people rich as well as poor were subject to taxation. It meant a considerable deduction from the amount of income earned by individuals and it affected the economic life to a great extent. In return for the taxes paid the people had the satisfaction that they were on the whole protected by their rulers and that the rulers made gifts of various kinds to help the cause of education and learning, to maintain irrigation works, temples and other important public institutions.

Trade and Industry

Even though agriculture was the main occupation of the people there were sections among them who carried on trade either as individuals or as members of merchant and trade guilds. Both inland and overseas trade flourished in the Kākatiya empire.

The record from Warangal mentions various articles brought to the capital for sale. The articles were rice, wheat, green-lentils, cholan, mustard, pepper, honey, kanugha oil, gingelly oil, ghee, turmeric, ginger, mangoes, bananas, maduphala, kammarenu, arecanuts, coconuts, rosaries (rudraksha) and even glass-beads (gāju-pūsa).

Gaṇapatidēva gave protection to foreign traders whose ships got wrecked on his shores. The abhayaśāsana of Gaṇapatidēva at Mōṭupalli assured such traders, that instead of confiscating their entire cargo, as was the previous practice, custom duties only were collected by the state[94]. Motupalli or Dasynyakkondapaṭṭana became a great centre of trade during the reign of Gaṇapatidēva.

Mōṭupalli was the Mutfile of Marcopolo. Here the merchants traded in precious gems like corals, ivory, pearl, etc. Diamonds, the largest and the brightest of its kind were exported to the countries like China[95]. Silk came from China and were known as Chinambaramu, Diamonds were mined in the Telugu land from ancient times. Marcopolo in his wonderment says that in the Kākatīya kingdom there were many mountains in which diamonds were found. On the mountains there was a multitude of serpents, both long and thick, so that those who went there did so in great fear.

In those days the present Guntur district was rich in diamonds. Kolluru (in the Sattenapalli taluk, Guntur district) was a very important place, where diamond mines were in operation. Probably these were the diamond mines visited by

Marcopolo in the 13th century.[76] Dyed and muslim linen was available abundantly at Machilipaṭnam and its neighbourhood. Woollen blankets and carpets were woven at Orugallu.[97]

The art of jewellery making was in flourishing condition. The jewellers called 'akkasālavaru' were a separate community by themselves. Their medium of artistic expression was not only gold and silver but ivory too.[98] Iron ore was produced at Kūnasamudramu near Nermala in the Warangal district. Salt was extracted from sea-water in coastal towns.[79]

Those working on metal were collectively known as 'Paṇchanamavaru' a corruption of the word 'Panchanamavaru' also known as the Viśvakarma kula, as they claimed descent from the five sons of Viśvakarama. They worked on gold, silver, iron, brass and bell-metal.[100] Each village was an industrial unit by itself and its artisans manufactured almost all the requirements. At Ōrugallu there were the smiths working on the five metals, silk-weavers, cotton-weavers (padmasali), mat-weavers (medara), painters, masons (uppara), potters, tailors (meravandlu), fishermen (bēsta), toddy tappers, bangle-makers, washer-men, shepherds, oil-crushers, toy-makers, those who prepared perfumed powders (bukka-vandlu) and makers of materials for transport of goods and corn.[101]

Coinage

A few coins attributed to Gaṇapatidēva, Ambadeva and Prataparudra have been cited. Epigraphs refer to coins called 'kēsari-gadya', 'kēsari-visa', 'mada', 'gandyana' and 'gokana-gaḍyana'.[102] The māda is also mentioned by *Śiddhēśvara charitra* along with the 'varaha' and 'suvarna'. The *Kreedabhīrāmaṁ* refers to the 'ruka' which was enough to procure a tasty meal at Ōrugallu.

The Kākatiya kingdom under Gaṇapatidēva appear to have been highly prosperous, in spite of the numerous wars waged and the consequent expenditure incurred. Land watered by the various irrigational works, paid good dividends. And people had abundant cattle and sheep. Industries flourished and trade, inland, and overseas, enriched the kingdom. The people lived happy and content under the benevolent rule of Gaṇapatidēva.

References

1. P.V. Parabrahma Sastry–*The Kakatiyas,* p. 281.
2. *E.I.*, XII, p. 183 ff. But curiously enough the Ekamranatha inscription credits Prōla–II, the grandson of Prola–I, with this achievement; *I.A.*, XII, p. 199 ff.
3. *C.T.I.*, II, p. 29.
4. *C.T.I.*, II, p. 24; *A.R.E.*, 31 of 1957-57; cf. *E.H.D.*, p. 678.
5. *Pratapa Charitra*, p. 31 ff.
6. *Ibid.*, pp. 40-48.
7. *E.H.D.*, Part IX, p. 678.
8. Yah prottumga-taramga-samgati-bhavad-dimdire-piṇḍa-cchalat—tire tara-ar-emdu-mayim malam sa-dorvadayan bramyam—mamdara-mamtha-mamthana-va-Sad—ek-emdu-sambutijam ksir-abdher—adharikaroti paritah kirt (t) im jagad-vyapinim–*C.T.I.*, Part II, p. 39, Vol. 2.
9. *H.A.S.*, No. 3.
10. *C.T.I.* Part II, p. 134 ff.
11. *Sivayogasaramu*, Subhashi, p. 22.
12. E.I., Ind. XXXVI, p. 217, v. 21.
13. *H.A.S.*, p. 24.
14. *Ibid.*, 70.
15. *Ibid.*, 102.
16. *C.T.I.*, II, p. 34.
17. *Ibid.*, pp. 69, 91, 93.
18. *C.T.I.*, II, p. 71.
19. *Ibid.*, p. 76.
20. *Ibid.*, p. 122.
21. *C.T.I.*, II, p. 109.
22. *S.I.I.*, X, p. 143.

23. *C.T.I.*, II, p. 24.
24. *M.A.S.I.*, No. 6, p. 1.
25. *J.A.H.R.S.*, VI., p. 239.
26. *H.A.S.*, No. 4.
27. *Ibid.*, No. 3.
28. For the details of the Bayyaram tank see *E.A.*, Vol. I, p. 71, No. 1.
29. *C.T.I.*, II, p. 152, ff.
30. *S.I.I.*, X, p. 207.
31. *E.H.D.*, X, p. 207.
32. *H.A.S.*, No. 18, Km. 10.
33. *Ibid.*, Km. 5.
34. *Ibid.*, Km. 10.
35. *S.I.I.*, Vol. X, p. 395.
36. *Ibid.*
37. *C.T.I.*, II, p. 49, v. 23.
38. *H.A.S.*, No. 18, No. 3.
39. *S.I.I.*, Vol. X, p. 475; S. 1215 (1294 A.D.).
40. *S.I.I.*, X, p. 340.
41. *C.T.I.*, II, p. 71.
42. *Pratapa Charitra*, p. 34.
43. *C.T.I.*, II, p. 133.
44. *H.A.S.*, No. 18, Mn. 5-8.
45. *H.A.S.*, No. 18, Mn. 24.
46. *S.I.I.*, IV, p. 1243.
47. *Ibid*, X, No. 482, *H.A.S.*. Km. 10.
48. *J.A.H.C.*, IV, p. 21.
49. *S.I.I.*, X, No. 5; 482, 488, 503.
50. *C.T.I.*, II, p. 89.
51. *S.I.I.*, X, p. 420.
52. *Ibid.*, No. 435.
53. *H.A.S.*, No. 18, Km. 10.
54. *S.I.I.*, X, No. 477.
55. *H.A.S.*, No. 18, Km. 5.
56. *Ibid.*, Mn. 5.

57. *S.I.I.*, X, No. 451.
58. *Ibid.*
59. *Ibid.*, No. 275.
60. *H.A.S.*, No. 18, Km. 6.
61. *H.A.S.*, p. 201.
62. *Ibid.*, p. 77, Vol. 16.
63. Asvasa II, v. 54.
64. *C.T.I.*, II, pp. 131-32.
65. *H.A.S.*, No. 18; wg. 18; *S.I.I.*, X, Nos. 295, 442, 468; *E.I.*, XIX, p. 163, v. 16.
66. *C.T.I.*, II, p. 61; *Bhimesvara Purana*, II, Vol. 56.
67. *C.T.I.*, II, p. 113.
68. *S.I.I.*, X, 427, 499, 509.
69. M. Somasekhara Sarma–*History of Reddi Kingdoms*, p. 363.
70. *S.I.I.*, X, No. 509; Penumuli Record of Prataparudra, dated 1314 A.D.
71. Kshetra Ganita–Andhra Sahitya Parisha Library, No. 1089.
72. S.I.I., Vol. X, No. 509, Penumali Record of Prataparudra.
73. *S.I.I.*, Vol. X, No. 395, Malkapuram. *C.T.I.*, Part II, No. 26 Mallecheruvu, Auzuranagar taluk, Nalgonda district.
74. *H.A.S.*, No. 4, Vol. 41—The Pakhal inscription of Ganapatideva. The land granted to the composer of the inscription is stated to be five nivartanas in the Sanskrit portion, and five martus in the Telugu portion of the record.
75. *N.D.I.*, Vol., C.P., No. 17, Vol. 28, p. 143—Sri M.S. Sarma corrects the 'Trimasti' (30) as 'Vimsati' (20) on the basis of Hemadri's *Chaturvarga Chintamani* which gives the sub-division of a nirvartana as equal to 20 dandas or 200 hastas, *History of the Reddi Kingdoms*, p. 367.
76. *C.T.I.*, II, No. 51.
77. *S.I.I.*, Vol. X, No. 810; *C.T.I.*, Part II, No. 26.
78. *C.T.I.*, Part II, No. 26, v. 19-21.
79. *S.I.I.*, Vol. X, Nos. 480, 468.
80. *E.H.D.*, Part. IX, p. 684.
81. *E.H.D.*, Part. IX, p. 684.
82. *A.R.E.*, C.P. 10 and 11 of 1918-19; *S.I.I.*, Vol. X, No. 473.

83. *E.H.D.*, Part IX, pp. 684-85.
84. *S.I.I.*, Vol. X, No. 473, Tripurantakam—This record is partly in Hale Kannada.
85. *C.T.I.*, Part II, No. 14 dated 1228 Warangal.
86. *S.I.I.*, Vol. X, No. 304.
87. *S.I.I.*, Vol. IV, No. 637.
88. *S.I.I.*, Vol. X, No. 427, D. 1270. Guntur District; No. 447, Kollu, Guntur District, D. 1279 A.D.
89. *C.T.I.*, Part, II No. 26, Mallecheruvu, Nalgonda district, No. 30.
90. *S.I.I.*, Vol. X, No. 358.
91. *S.I.I.*, Vol. X, No. 314.
92. *S.I.I.*, Vol. X, Nos. 427, 486.
93. *Ibid.*, No. 427.
94. The Motupalli inscription of Ganapatideva, D. 1244-45; *E.I.*, Vol. XII, Ed. by E. Hultzsch.
95. *Travels of Marcopolo.*
96. Gardon Meckenzie–*Krishna District Manual*, p. 71.
97. Suravaram Pratapa Reddi–Kakatiyulanati Sanghika Charitra, *Ka. San.*, p. 240; *Kr. Ra.*
98. *C.T.I.*, Part II, Nos. 30, 14; *Kr. Ra.*
99. Suravaram Pratapa Reddi of cit. p. 240.
100. *Sid. Cha.*, p. 151; *History of Reddi Kingdoms*, p. 380.
101. *Sid. Cha.* Introduction, pp. 76 ad 77; *C.T.I.*, Part II, No. 30.
102. The treasure hoard unearthed at Kavaiyadavalli in the Nellore district revealed a solitary gold coin of 56.25 grains in weight having a lion on the obverse and a legend, (ka) tigana in Telugu characters on the reverse. The Government Epigraphist feels that this coin confirms the existence of the coin 'Kesari-gadya' mentioned in the inscription from Bhattiprolu, *A.R.E.*, No. 295 of 1936-37. Also see Part II of the report, p. 655.

7

Genealogical Table of the Kakatiyas

Dūrjaya

|

Venna (founder of the Kākatīya line)

|

Gunḍa-I

|

Gunḍa-II

|

Gunḍa-III (who died some time before A.D. 900)

Eṛṛa

|

Betiya (mentioned in the Mangaḷḷu grant only)

|

Gunḍa-IV

|

Garuda (Bēta-I) (A.D. 996-1051)

|

Prōla-I (A.D. 1052-1076)

|

Trobuvanamalla Bēta (Bēta-II, A.D. 1076-1108)

|

- Tribhuvanamalla Dūrgarāja (A.D. 1108-1116)
- Prola-II (A.D. 1116-1157) m. Muppama
  - Rudra (A.D. 1158-1195)
  - Mahadeva m. Bayyama (A.D. 1196-1199)
    - Ganapatideva m. Somaladevi (A.D.1199-1262)
    - Mailaṁba
    - Kundaṁba
  - Harihara
  - Ganapati
  - Rēpolla Durga

Ganapaṁa m.Kota Beta

Rudramadēvi m. (A.D.1262-1289) Chāḷukya Vīrabhadra

Mummaḍaṁba m. (Kākati) Mahādēva

Rudrama m. Yadava Prince Ellanadēva

Ruyyama m. Induluri Annaya mantri

Pratāparudra (A.D. 1289-1323)

Kākatīya Kingdom Under Gaṇapatidēva

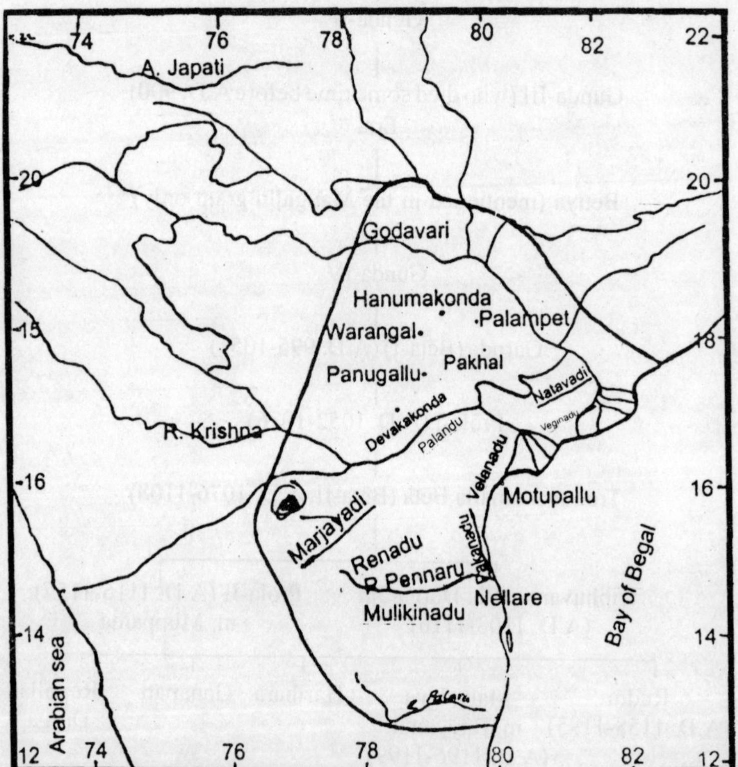

Note: Names which are underlined in the map indicate the territorial divisions.

Appendix

Relations between the Kakatiyas of Warangal and Yadavas of Devagiri

The Early Rulers of the Kakatiyas

The first member of the family was Venna. He is said to have born in the family of Durjaya. Some other ruling families of Andhradesa like the Venanadu Chiefs also claim their origin from Durjaya. But the historicity of any of these Durjayas cannot be established with certainty. The information about Venna, the founder of the Kakatiya family is that he ruled from the town Kakati, on account of which the members of his faimly were called Kakatiyas or the lords of Kakati. A.D. 800 to 815 to Venna. No information about Gunda I and Gunda II. We can place both of them between A.D. 815-865.

Gunda—III, Erra and Betiya

In the Masulipatam plates of Bhima I[1] we notice that his eldest son Irimarteganda killed a Rastrakuta general demdena Gunda in an engagement that took place at Paruvemguru. The Masulipatnam plates are not dated, but it is well known that Bhima I was contemporary of Krishna II (A.D.880-912). So Gunda III died at the hands of Chalukya Bhima's son Irimartiganga. Gkunda III was the earliest known member of the Kākatiya family who came to the Telugu country. The Kākatiya history begins with this event roughly datable to A.D. 895.

Gunda III was followed by Erra who according to the Bayyaram record was the ruler of Kurravadi in the present Mahbubabad taluk Warangal district. Kurravadi otherwise known as Karavi Krishna II might have annexed some part of the Karavi region and posted Erra as its governor, but Mudugonda Chalukyas occupied Karavi Kakatiya Chief rebreated into the interior.

According to the Mangallu grant Erra's son was Beteya, had no significant role in the family history.

Gunda—IV, C.A.D. 955-995

Beteya's son was Gunda IV. He earned a name among

the Rastrakuta generals and thereby a stronghold in the eastern borders of Telingana. We continued as a loyal subordinate of the Rastrakutas till their sudden collapse in A.D. 973. It was also the year when the Vengi ruler Danarnava was slain. Gunda with his Rastrakuta affliations was now in a dilemma whether to surrender himself to the new Chalukya. King Taila II or Jata Choda Bhima who sitted the Vengi kingdom after killing its rulers Danarnava.[2] He remained independent with small principaletes in the Karavi region. With the help of Tailapa II (Chalukya) Virizala Erra killed. Gunda in a battle and reinstated Bettu Beta at Koravi. Here comes to an end of the Rastrakuta subordination of the early Kakatiyas.

Beta I.C. A.D. 1000—1052

The Bayyaram inscription states that Beta made Anumakonda his capital. Which is supported by Gudur epigraph Beta settled as a subordinate of the Western Chalukya king. Beta Anumakonda as capital. From the statement of the Kazipet Darga inscription[3] of Durgaraja, he is credited with the title Chola-Chanu-Vardhi-Premathana, that is who churned the ocean of the Chola armies he participated in the Chalukya invasions against Cholas.

Prola I: A.D. 1052—1076

Prola I, a Chieftain who was holding a fief hardly equal to a modern taluk in area, cannot be supposed to have conducted on his own accord; but they must have been only on behalf of his overlord Trailokyamalla Someswara. Prola I participated in the campaign of Yuvaraja Vikramaditya on Konkan and Chakrakuta.

Among the local chiefs whom he conquered and slew in the battle were Annaya, son of Kadparti Durga who was the chief of the region and Gonna, the Purukuta chief of Gunasagara. Prola I who obtained Anumakonda—Vishaya as permanent fief from King Trailokyamalla. Prola I adopted

Varaha as their insignia. He constructed a tank called Kesaritataka.

Beta II: C.A.D. 1076—1108

This Beta's earliest record is found at Anumakonda which is dated A.D. 1079[4]. Here this chief credited with the title Sriman Vikrama-Chakri Sri Beta-manddalikottamah. It indicates that he started his career some time before this date almost simultaneously with his overlord Vikramaditya VI whose accession took place in A.D. 1076.

Four epigraphs of this Beta have come to light, they were Anumakonda inscription, Sanigraram epigraph. His other records are the Banajipet epigraph.

Durgaraja

Durgaraja succeeded his father Beta II in about A.D. 1108. Durgaraja ruled upto 1117. Within ten years after Beta II, his second son Prola II was in power as seen in the latter's Padmakshi temple inscription of A.D. 1117. If Durgaraja ever ruled, it is to be supposed that it took place between these two dates namely A.D. 1108 and 1117. The unpublished Kottapalli epigraph in the Nalgonda district of the time of Ganapatideva offers a clue to what might have happened in this record, it states, was so benevolant that he protected even his bhratrivya, that is his brother's son who sought asylum. Prola's action of depriving Durgaraja of his legitimate right was sanctioned not only by the King but also by the spiritual guru. Kakati Beta II his son Durgaraja died between A.D. 1107 and A.D. 1117. Prola II ruled between A.D. 1116—1157. Prola's succession was not altogether peaceful. The political disturbances that took place in Telingana during the preceding decade beginning from A.D. 1106, owing to the revolutionary attitude of the Paramara Jaggadeva. He strove hard with unsparing efforts to uphold the Supreme authority of the Chalukya King Jagadekamalla II in Telingana.

Prola II, according to an epigraph at Daksharamam[5] was slain by Chodayaraja of the Kota family and the Haihaya Chiefs Satya and Mallideva of the Kona country. A Suryavamsa Chief named Mahadevaraja claims for himself the credit of killing Prola. However Prola II was killed in battle probably in his attempt to conquer the Coastal Andhra-desa.

What kind of conditions prevailed in Telingana before the Kakatiyas and at the time of establishment of Kakatiya Kingdom are discussed in the following paras.

The history of the Kakatiyas begins from the closing part of the tenth century. They emerged as Sovereign power before A.D. 1163. Till then they were the subordinates of the Rastrakutas and the Western Chalukuyas of Kalyana successively. During this period the sphere of their activity being in Telingana of the present Andhra Pradesh state their dealings were directly connected with the other subordinate families of the region. Among them three feudatory families surrounding the Kakatiya. Principality, namely the Chalukyas of Mudigonda in the east, the Polavasa Chiefs in the north-west, and the Telugu Choda Chiefs of Kanduru in the South deserve consideration. The relations of the above chiefs with the Kakatiyas were more or less hostile.

Starting Mudugonda Chalukyas independent political career in the Mudugonda region near Khammam in about 8th century they were in possession of the region including Koravi for a long period till the end of twelfth century. Between the powerful Kingdom of the Eastern Chalukyas and the Rastrakutas and subsequently the Western Chalukyas of Kalyana they could retain their individuality as subordinates. But when the Kakatiyas emerged as independent power in Telingana they were forced to leave their ancestral principality and seek shelter in the Coastal region. Their relation with the

Kakatiya Chiefs was very limited only in the beginning and after becoming independent, the Kakatiyas had to fight with them. In the intervening period there seems to have been practically no interference in each other's affairs.

Like the Mudugonda Chiefs those of Polavasa also played an important role during the time of the early Kakatiyas. Their headquarters Polavasa in the modern Polas in the Jagtial taluk of Karimnagar district to the North of Warangal.

Both the families of the Kakatiyas and Medaraja belonged to the same stock of Rastrakuta generals of rank and settled in Telingana as their subordinates. Subsequent to the fall of the Rastrakuta power the Chalukyas allowed them to continue as Mahamandalesvaras with their respective fiefs adjacent to each other. Though cordial in the beginning their relations after some time were far from friendliness. Finally Medaraja, as it seems joined hands with the rivals of the Chalukya King Bhulokamalla and revolted for independece. King Jagadekamalla II soon after his accession led in expedition to put down the rebellions in Telingana. Prola II and Rudra taking advantage of the disloyal behaviour of Meda and his brother Gumda stood by the side of Jegadekamalla II and suppressed the revolt by killing Gumda and making Meda II flee from his Principality.

The Chodas of Kanduru ruled over Kandurunadu comprising present Jadcharla and Acchampet taluks in the Mahbubnagar district and the Nalgonda and Miryalaguda taluks of Nalgonda districts Konduru and Panugallu as their capitals from about A.D. 1060 to 1160.

The actual history of these Chiefs with reference to the Kakatiyas begins from Tomdaya II, the eldest son of Bhima II. The next phase in the history of these Chiefs is connected with the Kakatiya Chiefs Prola II on one occasion and his son Rudra at a later stage.

After passing through the semi-independent state which

they enjoyed for nearly two decades Gokarna's son Udayachoda the only remaining Chief of this family honourably acknowledged the supremacy of Kakati Rudra who by then was an independent ruler. As subordinate of the Kakatiyas they virtually became politically insignificant. The members of the family continued for pretty a long period simply enjoyed their fiefs.

Mahamandaleswara Paramara Jagaddeva a prince of the Paramar royal family of Malwa was its Governor from A.D. 1104 to 1108. The region to the West of Anumkonda-Vishaya was in those days under the direct control of the Chalukya Kings. It was administered the Viceroys of the rank of Mahamandaleswara with their Capital Kollipaka.

According to his Kolanupaka inscription Jagaddeva was the son of Udayaditya and grandson of Gondala, the Pitrivya or Paternal uncle of Bhoja. After Bhoja his son Jayasimha succeeded to the throne of Malwa in about A.D.1054. During his reign Malwa was invaded by Karna, a Chalukya King of Gujarat. Then Udayaditya with the help of Vikramaditya VI managed to capture the throne and ruled upto A.D. 1081 when his eldest son Lakshmade succeeded to the throne. Being much impressed with the good qualities of prince Jagaddeva, the Chalukya King Vikramaditya brought him to his court and treated him with fatherly affection. He was offered the Governorship of Kollipaka for about 4 years.

The Sanigaram record refers itself to the prosperous reign of Chalukya Tribhuvanamalladeva and mentions Mahamandaleswara Kakati Betarasa the lord of Anumakundapura. It states that Kamdamayya the dandanayaka of Mahamandalesvara Jagaddevarasa made on the occasion of the lunar eclipse occurred in the 15th day of Magha, Thursday in the year Vyaya, Saka 1022, mistake for 1028 (10th January A.D. 1107) a gift of some land to the God Bhimesvaradeva of

Sanigaram included in Sabbinadu. The position of Jagaddeva, that is relation to that of Beta is not explicit. Perhaps he was holding Kollipaka 7000 excluding Sanigaram and its contiguous villages. The Anumakonda region was bestowed on Kakati Prola as permanent fief by Trailokyamalla Somesevara I. The statement of the Padmakshi temple inscription of Beta's III son Prola I that with the statesmanship of his minister Vaija–damdadhipa Beta II could secure Sabbi-Sayira clearly indicates that this region of Jagaddeva was transferred to Beta. The reason for Kumara Somesvara's visit to Vemulavada in the preceding year must have been connection with this change of territory. Its immediate reaction was his difference with the King. There must have been something else which made the King prefer Beta to Jagaddeva for bestowing Sabbi-1000 on the former: perhaps the King at once appointed his son Kumara Somesvara as the Viceroy of Kollipaka-7000 and Jagaddeva was forced to leave Telingana. This situation helped Beta II in getting back not only the Singaram area but even the whole of Sabbinadu—1000.

Deprived of his position, Jagaddeva retaliated against the Kakatiyas making alliance with the Polava a Chief. It seems quite possible that Jagaddeva, conspiring with these Chiefs made an attack on Anumakonda, the capital of his immediate enemies, the Kakatiyas. But he was utterly defeated by Beta's son Prola II, which event has been eulogised in the Anumakonda record of Rudradeva. We are not certain whether Beta II was alive or not at that time.

The Early Rulers of the Yadavas

Seunachandra I. Yadavas also had their ancestral history. Seunachandra I is the earliest member of the family. The Sangamaner epigraph states that the territory which he ruled came to be known after him[6]. Hemadri confirms this[7]. The statement in the Dalali plate viz., Yan-akaripuram Cha

Seunapuram Sri-Sindinerevari reveals that he built the city of Seunapura in the Sindinera area approximately he ruled between 835 A.D. and 860 A.D. Amoghavarsha I Nripatunga (Rastrakuta) was then the Suzerain.

Dhadiyappa I C. 860-885 A.D., Bhillama I C. 885-910 A.D. and Rajugi c. 910-935 A.D. approximately they ruled between this period.

Vaddiga I (c. 935-970 A.D.). Sangamaner epigraph is the only source which gives some information about the next ruler Vaddaga I. It states that he was 'follower of Krishnaraja' which may be interpreted to mean that he was subordinate of Krishnaraja, i.e., Rastrakutakrishna III. Krishna III ruled between A.D. 939 and 967. Vaddiga's have started his career earlier Vaddiga's period may thus be fixed as c. 935 to 970 A.D.

Bhillama II (c. 970-1005 A.D.). Bhillama II, successor of Vaddagi I withnessed major changes in the political situation of the Deccan. After Krishna III the Rastrakuta power became weak and soon after, i.e., in 1973 A.D., it was overthrown by Chalukya Taila II. It is seen from the Sangamaner record that Bhillama in due course accepted the Chalukya authority.

Bhillama II, stationed as the Governor of Seunadesa which was the Northern frontier of the Chalukya territory, had a special responsibility to bear. He protects the frontier from Paramaras. It is stated in the Sangamaner record that he killed the Paramara King Munja. This indeed is a tall claim for we know that Munja was imprisoned and later killed by Taila II[8]. Bhillama queen Lakshmi, belonged to Rastrakuta family. The Seuna queen proved herself to be worthy ruler and that her achievement was appreciated by three royal families.

Vesugi I (c. 1005-1010 A.D.). The next ruler was Vesugi I. We have no information about him. No record of him is discovered.

Bhillama III (c. 1010-1055 A.D.). Vesugi I was succeeded by his son Bhillama III in about 1010 A.D. Bhillama III from the beginning developed a hostile attitude towards the Chalukya rulers and tried to extricate himself from his feudatory ties. But he repeatedly failed.

Bhillama's last date is uncertain. He was succeeded by two members of the family who had together a short period of rule. Next came Seunachandra II whose earliest known date is 1069 A.D.[9]

Vesugi II (c. 1055-1068 A.D.). Bhillama III was succeeded by his younger son Vesugi II, Vesugi II had a short reign after Vesugi II, his son Bhillama-IV tried to usurp power, setting aside the claim of Seunachandra, who was the legitimate successor, but Seunachandra vanguished the forces of Bhillama IV.

Seunachandra II (c. 1068-1080 A.D.). In his struggle to get back his thorne, Seunachandra II appear to have taken the help of the Silahara Chief Bhoja. Seunachandra sided and helped the Vikramaditya VI. Hemadri explicitly avers that Seunachandra placed Paramardhi, i.e., Vikramaditya VI on the Kalyana throne[10]. As a reward for his service, more territory was added to the Seuna fiefdom. The Davalali plates associate him with the Governance of the territory to the South of River Narmada.

Airammadeva (c. 1080-1110 A.D.). Seunachandra II had two sons, Airamma and Singhana I and the former succeeded him. The only historical information available about him is that he defeated the Chalukya King. Bhuvanaikamalla Somesvara II and secured the kingdom for Vikramaditya VI.

Singhana I (c. 1110-1145 A.D.). Airammadeva was succeeded by his brother Singhana I. He deservedly bore the title Sahasanka. Inscriptions speak of his many victories. In this context mention is made of his successes against the Kings of Karnata[12], and Gurjara. Hemadri credits Singhana with bringing the elephant Karpuratilaka from Lamjipura and completing the decoration of the Karpuravana of Paramardi (Vikramaditya VI).[13] Singhana had a fairly long rule.

Mallugi I, Amaragangageya and Govindaraja (c. 1145-1155 A.D.). Singhana I was succeeded by Mallugi I. Mallugi's son Amaragangageya and his son Govindaraja. The rule of these three princes was uneventful and must have been short as well.

Mallugi II (c. 1155-1165 A.D.). The political conditions in the Chalukya kingdom were now fast change. Taila II lost his ground on account of the aggressive activities of his Kalachuri subordinate Bijjala II. The Seunas took advantage of this situation to assert their independence. Mallugi II, with whom the Seunas can be said to have entered into the arena of the struggle for supremacy, refused to accept the suzeranity of the Kalachuri Bijjala II and challenged his authority as is evidenced by the Suktimuktavali of Jalhana.

Mallugi clashed with the Kakatiyas also. The Anumakonda inscription of Kakatiya Rudradeva[14] states that thus Kings defeated Mallugi. This Mallugi must be identical with Seuna Mallugi II.

To Mallugi goes the credit of mobilising the military strength of the Seunas and making a bid for sovereignty in the confused political conditions by the Kalachuri upsurge. Though his efforts did not bear fruit immediately, he paved the way for the success of his son Bhillama V.

Kaliyaballala and his Son (c. 1165-1173 A.D.)

The next rulers according to Hemadri, was Kaliyaballala, the elder of the two sons of Mallugi II. But within a few years his young brother Bhillama V who was powerful and ambitious wrested the kingdom, after Kaliyaballala from his son, whose name is not known.

At the time of the establishing of the Sovereign Kingdom of Yadavas prevailing conditions are discussed as follows :

Karnataka before the Seunas and at the time of establishing of the independent kingdom preliminary to commencing our study of the history of the Seunas, it is necessary to understand the political conditions that prevailed in Karnataka and around on the eve of their rise to power.

The latter half of the twelfth century was a period of conflict and confusion in the political history of Karnataka. The supremacy of the Western Chalukyas of Kalyan, who held sway over this region and beyond for about two centuries, was on the wane. This provided opportunities for the feudatory rulers and subordinate Chiefs to defy their overlords and set up their independent rule.

The Kalchuris who originally hailed from central India had settled in Northern Karnataka about the tenth century. They gained prominence before the end of the eleventh century when Jogama (1080-1118 A.D.) established himself as a Mahamandaleswar under Chalukya VikramadityaVI (1076-1126 A.D.). The Kalachuris had matrimonial alliances with Chalukyas of Kalyani. The process of usurpation was started in 1156 A.D. during the rule of Taila III (1151-1162 A.D.) and completed in 1162 A.D., Jogama's grandson Bijjala II, offspring of a further reciprocal marriage alliance, planned to seize power during the subsequent weak regime of his suzerains.

The protagonists of the Chalukya sovereignty rallied round Somesvara IV, Taila III's son and successor, and succeeded in terminating the usurpers rule (1184 A.D.). But this king was incapable of arresting the forces of disintegration and his empire in no time vanished like mist before the storm.

By this time, the Northern areas of the Chalukya dominions were threatened with occupation by the growing might of Bhillama of the Seuna family. Kalachuri usurpation, fell of easy prey to the increasing pressure of this ambitious Chief. Somesvara IV could never establish his hold on this ancestral capital. By about 1186 A.D. he retired to Jayantipura and somehow maintained semblance of his rule for a few years with the support of Kadamba feudatories of the area until 1200 A.D.

A loyal feudatories of the Chalukyas, the Hoyasalas rose rapidly to power in the Southern part of their dominions. If Vinayaditya (1047-1098 A.D.) contributed to enhance the power and prestige of his overlords by his faithful services his grandson Vishnuvardhana (1108-1152 A.D.) aspired to setup his independent rule in defiance of his mighty suzerain Vikramaditya. But he miserably failed in his attempt. His grandson Ballala I when he commenced his rule (1173-1220 A.D.). At this time the Chalukya sovereignty was tottering with the aggression of the Kalachuri usurpers. Though his inroads in the Northern parts of the Chalukya empire met with only temporary success, the independent rule of the Hoyasala dynasty in the South became a fait accompli.

The Hoyasalas had as their rivals the Seunas in the north. The position of the minor feudatories during this period of transition was quite uncertain. This is indicated by the epigraphical record which some times do not mention any sovereign ruler at all with reference to the petty ruling Chiefs of particular regions. In some other records the overlords are mentioned in a conflicting manner: for instance, if he is a Seuna in one, a Hoyasala or a Chalukya in another. This reflects the confuse political situation of the period.

The neighbouring states Malwa, Gujarat and Andhra. The impacts created by them in the political atmosphere of Karnataka were some closer and some times remote.

The Paramaras of Malwa, the Chalukyas of Kalyana and the Chalukyas of Gujarat, whose territories were adjacent to one another, often engaged themselves in mutual feuds. The Paramara enmity was now directed against the Seunas who had campaigned against them as the vassals of Chalukyas. Paramaras had in the Chalukyas of Gujarat another formidable adversity.

The Chalukyas,who had reached the heights of glory in the days of Jayasimha Siddharajas (1094-1143 A.D.) subsequently lost their importance weakened by frequent incursions of the Muslim invaders, their power declined.

On the Eastern border came to prominence the Kakatiyas of Warangal who earlier owed their allegiance to the Eastern Chalukyas of Vengi, when the latter lost their individuality, they transferred their loyalty to the mighty Chalukyas of Kalyana, serving them as their faithful feudatories for some time. Their ambition to become independent received impetus at the time of Prola II (1117-1163 A.D.) who was a powerful prince. Exploiting the political siuation in the reign of the Western Chalukya King Taila III, who was hard pressed by the rise of the Kalachuri usurper Bijjala II, this Kakatiya ruler defied and defeated his overlord in an encounter (1162 A.D.).

The conflicts between the Sovereign kingdom of the Kakatiya and the Yadava of Devagiri re-discussed in the following :

The Kakatiyas ruled Telingana more or less two centuries as sovereign kings with Warangal as their capital. The Yadavas of Devagiri ruled more than 125 years as sovereign kings.

Rudra came into conflict with the Seunas of Devagiri in the last year of his reign. It has as yet proved impossible to ascertain the circumstances in which this conflict arose whether Rudra, in an attempt to expand his territory Westwards, invaded the Seuna Kingdom, or whether it was the Seunas who, hoping to curb his growing power, first attacked him, are questions which we are unable to answer for lack of information.

The real struggle between sovereign kings of Rudradeva of Kakatiya and Bhillama V of Yadava began during their reign.

Kakati Rudradeva A.D. 1158-1195 : His Contemporary Yadava Kings were Bhillama V A.D. 1173-1192. Jaitugi II A.D. 1199-1200

Prola II was succeeded by his eldest son Rudradeva some time before Saka 1080 (A.D. 1158) the date of the Daksharamam inscription of his minister Inangala Brammireddi.[15] In addition to the Saka year 1080 the record mentions the 13th regnal year of the Chalukya–Chola Rajaraja II which need not be seriously considered.

The Thousand Pillar temple (Anumakonda) inscription[16] as in the case of Prola II, gives us a detailed account of Rudra's military achievements also, which in fact justify the proclamation of Kakatiya Sovereignty.

Rudra's contemporary of Yadava king Bhillama V (1173-1192 A.D.). Hemadri, the only authority to speak of Bhillama's seizing of power, obviously approves of his action, when he states that after Kaliyaballala, Yaduvamsa-Lakshmi left the son of Kaliyaballala and went to Bhillama, since she (i.e. Lakshmi) was enamoured of virtues. This much appears to be certain, that after the short rule of Kaliyaballala, Bhillama forcibly ousted Kaliyaballala's son and usurped the throne. He became sovereign ruler in 1186 A.D. but records are not unanimous in fixing the initial year Bhillama's assumption of sovereign power.

Basing on a verse in Jalhana's Suktimuktavali some scholars hold the view that Rudra was once defeated by the Yadava King Bhillama who ruled between A.D. 1173 and 1192. The relevant portion in the verse reads 'Vijita-bhur-Babhru-rana prangane which they interpreted that (Bhillama) conquired (some) territory in the battle field of Babhru. According to Dr. P.B. Desai the word Babhru was meant for (Kakati) Rudra as that word is a synonym to Rudra (Siva). But in the absence of other evidence this interpretation is doubtful[17]. It is more likely that the word Babhru is a Sanskritized place name. The earliest reference to the Seuna victory over the Kakatiyas is noticed in the Patna inscription of the reign of Singhana who ruled between A.D. 1200 and 1247[18]. Singhana's father Jaitrapala is stated in that record to have put to an end to the pleasure of the beloved ones of the ladies of Andhra. But the reference is not specific whether the Andhra King represented as the enemy of Jaitrapala was Rudra or his successor Mahadeva. The latter's death at the hands of the same Yadava King there is absolutely no evidence in the Kakatiya records. The other evidence brought forth in this connection is the citation from Hemadri, the Sri Karanadhipa of Yadava Mahadeva and his nephew Rama Chandra who states in the Vratakhanda of his Chaturvarga-Chintamani that Jaitrapala assumed the sacrificial vow on the holy ground of the battle field, throwing a great Kings into the fire of his prowess by means of laddles in the form of weapons offered a human sacrifice by immolating a victim in the shape of Rudra, the Tillingadhipati and thus vanquished the three worlds.[19] Here also we find the name of Jaitrapala's enemy as Rudra and which has been amended by R.G. Bandarkar and others as Raudara and it has been accepted by the subsequent writers[20]. But in the absence of corroborating evidence it is difficult to accept the amended version of Hemadri's statement. Even this subsequent eulogy does not mention Mahadeva's death at the hands of Jaitugi with event is borne out by more than one evidence. Hence it seems reasonable to believe that Hemadri's original statement Raudrasya Rudrakritch intends only Mahadeva and not Rudra as Bhandarkar thinks. But the word 'Raudra' is applicable to Rudra's son and not brother. Hemadri is not altogether definite in his statement whether the intended victim was Rudra's son or brother; Son, of course he did not have. But Ganapati who in the Upparapalli epigraph of Katayanayaka[21] is stated to be the son of Rudra probably by adoption also accompanied Mahadeva in his campaign on the Yadavas and it is possible that Hemadri out of confusion used the word Rudra (son of Rudra) for Mahadeva. Thus in the circumstances, supporting evidence alone is to be considered as deciding factor. Rudra's death at Jaitugi's hands is not known otherwise and therefore Hemadri's statement is not straight away believable. His last known date according to the inscription at Bekkallu, in the Jangaon Taluk, Warangal district is Saka 1117, Rakshana, Vaisakha Pornima corresponding to A.D. 1195, April 26.[22]

During the rule of Bhillama, the Seuna territory expanded considerably. The Narmada remained the northern boundary and south of that river, the whole of Maharashtra state barring Konkana, the northern areas of the present Mysore state viz. Bijapur, Belgaum, Bidar, Gulbarga and Raichur districts were included in his territory and the Malaprabha became the Southern boundary.

Mahadeva (A.D. 1195-1199). His Contemporary Yadava Ruler was Jaitugi (A.D. 1192-1199-1200)

As Rudra had no issues his younger brother Mahadeva succeeded him. Jaitugi's earliest known date is December 1192 A.D. He must have ascended the throne some time before that. Some of his records which are dated in his regnal years indicate that his rule commenced from an earlier date. Bhillama V's son Jaitugi. Bhillama thought it fit to associate his son with the administration of the kingdom.

According to the Khamdavalli copper plate grant of Prataparudara[23] Rudra gave the kingdom to his younger brother Mahadeva perhaps as regent of the young prince Ganapati. We have only two of this king one from Sundella in the Peddapalli taluk, Karimnagar district dated A.D. 1197[24] and another, a broken and undated record, in the Warangal fort[25]. The only political event of his reign which we know for plates state figuratively that while plundering the enemy's town he slept on the two temples of the elephant, stained with blood as if smeard with the red sandal of the breasts of the Goddess of victory[26] in the night. A similar statement occurs in the Yenamala inscription dated A.D. 1249-50[27]. The inscriptions of the Seunas also while describing the victories of those kings refer to this event. The Andhra King referred to in the Patna inscription of Singhana II (A.D.1200-47)[28] in connection with the victory of Jaitrapala as explained before, was Mahadeva but not Rudra. The paithan copper plate grant of Ramachandra states that Jaitrapala slew the king of Trikalinga a mistake for Trilinga, in a battle and rescued Ganapati from the prison and made him king[28]. On the basis of these and the literary evidence of Pratapa-Charitra and Somadevarajiya it can be definitely said that Mahadeva, invaded the Yadava country during the reign of Jaitugi II (A.D. 1192-1200) and in an attempt to seize the enemy's capital perished while fighting seated on an elephant in the night time. The circumstances which provoked Mahadeva to undertake this singular military enterprise are not known. The course of events that followed however indicate that the Yadava king did not entertain bitter enemity with the Kakatiyas, because according to the Bahal inscription of Singhana[30] Jaitugi an ocean of compassion made Ganapati whose life he saved in battle, lord of the Andhra country.

Ganapatideva (A.D. 1199-1262). His Contemporary Yadava Rulers were Jaitugi or Jairapala (A.D. 1192-1200) Simhana (A.D. 1200-1247) and Krishna (A.D. 1246-1260)

The earliest record of this king is the Manthena epigraph dated 26th December 1999[31] which seems to be of his first regnal year. Ganapatideva was the greatest king of the Kakatiya dynasty. He reigned for sixty-three years. His reign is considered as one of the most epochs in the history of the Andhra country. He was a very ambitious king. In implementing his imperialistic designs he came into conflict with some of the major powers of South India in general and that of Deccan in particular.

The Kalegaon plates of Mehadeva dated A.D. 1260 record that "Jaitugi the abode of compassion, liberated Ganapatideva from the prison and with great honour handed over him the earth"[32]. The paithan grant of Yadava Ramachandra refers that Jaitugi took Ganapati from prison and cause him to smile[33], sympathy, generosity and the aggressive policy of the Hoyasala Ballala (A.D. 1173-1220) may be the causes for liberation of Ganapatideva. According to P.V. Parabrahmasastry the circumstances under which Ganapatideva was set free and reinstated on the thron by the Yadava king Jaitugi are not definitely known[34]. An inscription at Belur records "moistening his vallant sword with the blood of his enemy, the Pandya king, he (Ballala II) whetted it on the grind stone the head of Bhillama and sheathed in the mouth of Jaitugi."[35] Ballala II defeated on Jaitrasimha in the battle at Saratur. Majority of the scholars including Dr. Kielhorn suggest that Jaithrasimha may be identified with Bhillama's son[36]. If this be so Jaitugi took an important part in the battle at Saratur. After this conquest Ballala is often found residing at Lokkagundi[37] (Lakkundi), the latest date of his residing there being A.D.1199 and A.D.1203[38]. Therefore Jaitugi probably desired to secure himself against an attack from the East in the event of a conflict with Hoyasalas in the South by making Ganapatideva as the king of the earth.

Jaitugi was succeeded by his son Simhana about A.D. 1210. He was the most important and powerful ruler among the Yadavas. It is stated in some of the Yadava inscription that Simhana defeated the king of Andhra. The Purushottamapuri plates[39] of Yadava Ramachandra dated Saka 1232 (A.D. 1310) record that Simhana defeated the Andhra King. The Editor of the plates identified the Andhra king defeated by Simhana with Ganapatideva of the Kakatiya dynasty.[40] The Uddhari and Ambey inscriptions describe him as the uprooter of the water-lily that was the head of the Telang king.[41] Another inscription dated A.D. 1217 states that Simhana defeated and restored the Telunga-Raya.[42] But a similar exploit of this kind is mentioned in connection with Krishna—the eldest grandson of Simhana. The Mamdapur[43] and Arjunvad[44] inscriptions of Krishna dated Saka 1172 and 1182 style him as, Tailamga-Maya-Sthapanacharya and Telunga-raya-Sthapana-charya respectively. The Yadava king who imprisoned and liberated Ganapatideva was Jaitugi and not Simhana and Krishna. So it is doubtful if they really came into conflict and defeated the Andhra king.

Recent writers on the subject suggested that Ganapatideva came into conflict with the Yadavas while fighting on behalf of Telugu-Choda Tikka I[45]. It is even supposed that Simhana, with his armies accompanied by Hoyasala Somesvara III invaded the Telugu-Choda kingdom. Simhana was vanquished and his armies were routed in the encounter[46]. The arguments appear to be wrong Tikka I is said in a inscription at little-Conjeevaram as 'Cataclysmic fire to the Ocean, viz; Kalyanpuri and the lord of Vikramasimhapuri[47]. The Nirvachanottara-Ramayanam states that Tikka captured the horse of one Lakumayya when he marched against Gurumuluru[48]. Ketana's Dasakumaracharitra informs us that he destroyed, Sevuna-Kataka-Samanta.[49] Coming all these evidences some scholars opined that Tikka I defeated Simhana.[50] Tikka's attack on Kalyanapuri or Kalyana most probably represents his conflict with the Hoyasalas and not Yadavas.

The Ekamranath inscription of Saka 1172[51] mentions one Simhana who is said to have been afraid of King

Ganapatideva. Most probably Simhana of our record refers to Singaladeva who was ruling the Ongole taluk of Guntur district. In the early records of Singaladeva there is no mention of his overlord. But the Chandalur inscription of A.D. 1253 refers Ganapatideva as ruling and Singaladeva as his subordinate[52]. It is probable that Singaladeva towards the close of his reign suffered a reverse at the hands of the Kakatiyas.[53]

A.S. Altakar states that Ganapatideva "Participated in the northern campaigns of Simhana, for one of his inscription, dated A.D. 1228 states that he had defeated the Latas." This claim can be explained only on the assumption that he had accompanied the Yadava forces in one of their Gujarat. In the inscription above referred Ganapati is seen to be content to assume the titles of an ordinary feudatory Chief, but later in his reign he succeeded in effecting a considerable Southward expansion of his Kingdom and began to feel strong enough to assume an independent status[54]. This argument is not sound for the title 'Mahamandalesvara' not only found in the Warangal inscription of A.D. 1228 where the conquest of Lata by Ganapatideva is referred to, but also noticed him many other records of him issued before and after that date.[55] In some cases the titles 'Chalamarit-ganda; and Muru-rayajagaddala', are also associated with the name of Ganapatideva[56]. The Pakahal[57] and Chebrolu[58] inscriptions inform us that the kings of Madra, Panchala, Videha, Kasi, Malava, Korala, Tummana, Nepala, Arimarda, Saka, Huna, and Hammira were supplicants at the door of Ganapatideva. It is not known whether he actually defeated the kings and annexed their kingdom referred to in the above inscriptions. Some of them viz: Magadha, Madra, Panchala, Videha, Kuru, and Kasi disappeared long before the time of Ganapatideva. The inclusion of these countries among the princes who came to pay homage to Ganapatideva may be attributed to literary convention popular with the

Prasastikaras of the period. We need not take therefore the conquest of late as a sober fact of history.

An inscription carved in the Southern wall of the second Prakara of the Nataraja temple at Chidambaram mentions one Kshoma or Kshemasura, defeated by Jatavarman Sundara-Pandya in connection with the Seunas- 'Kshemais-samam-Seunaih'[59]. Sri Mallampalli Somasekharasarma suggested on the strength of the phrase, 'Ganapati Kshemasura', occurring in a fragmentary record on a temple at Tirupatithat Kshema was none other than the Kakatiya Ganapatideva[60]. It is further supposed that Ganapatideva and the Seuna king joined forces and attempted to check the expansion of the Pandyan power[61]. The identification of Kshema with Ganapatideva appears to be a possible suggestion but at present in lacks support. The Tripurantakam inscription, dated in the 7th year of Maravarman-vikrama Pandya styles him as 'Kshemasura-vidarna-narasimha.'[62] The actual significance of these titles and phrases is veiled in obscurity.

Simhana and Krishna, the successors of Jaitugi also claimed themselves that they defeated and established the Andhra King in some of their inscriptions. This would probably mean that they either participated in Jaitugi's war against the Kakatiyas or merely inherited the titles from their predecessor Jaitugi.

Ganapatideva's relations with the Seunas were normally amicable throughout his long reign. Ganapati gave asylum to the Seuna princes and appointed them in his service. Certain Permadideva, son of Singhana is noticed in an inscription at Peruru in the Nalgonda district dated A.D. 1157 where in he is stated to have made gifts of lands to brahmanas all over the country ruled by Ganapatideva.[63] In his southern campaign against the Pandyas Ganapati was assisted by some Arya or Yadava chiefs as commanders of his armies.

Rudramadevi (A.D. 1262-89). Her Contemporary Yadava Rulers were Mahadeva A.D. 1261-1271. His Son Amana 1271 : Ramachandra A.D. 1271-1312.

Ganapati, who had no male issues nominated his daughter Rudramadevi as heir to the kingdom which she began to rule as Co-regent from A.D. 1259-60 under the name of Rudradeva Maharaja. Those were the days when the Kakatiya armies suffered defeat in the battle-field of Muttukur at the hands of the Pandyas. Although Ganapatideva ultimately managed to repel the invasion which penetrated as far as the river Krishna, he had to forfeit his hold over the southern territories, the succession of a lady to the throne was not met with the approval of some of her kinsmen and nobles. According to Pratapacharitra, certain chiefs named Harihara and Murarideva, Ganapati's sons by other queens, revolted against Rudrama and have seized the capital. It may be true to some extent, as it was against the Hindu Law for a lady to ascend the throne. But she could manage to tide over the difficulty and seize the throne with the help of some loyal supporters.

Mahadeva was associated with the administration of the kingdom in the capacity of the heir-apparent or Yuvaraja from the early part of Kannara or Krishna's rule.

Before she consolidated her position, a serious threat to the capital from the north. The Seuna king Mahadeva invaded the kingdom and the capital Orugallu. It is stated in Mahadeva's inscriptions that he captured the ruler of the Telinga country and his elephants. Hemadri the renowned scholar of the Yadava court states in his Vratakhanda that his master Mahadeva was credited with the title 'Tilunguraya-sirah Kamala-mulotpatana' that is the remover of the head of the Telungaraya. But a close examination reveals that it was borne by Jayatugi as well, who had really killed Mahadeva in A.D. 1198. So far as Yadava Mahadeva is concerned the title may be taken as hereditary. In order to enhance the greatness of his master Hemadri attributed to him the credit which belonged to his ancestor. But Mahadeva's invasion of the Kakatiya kingdom was a fact. According to the 17th century literary work Pratapacharitra, the Yadava king Mahadeva invaded the Kakatiya kingdom and laid seize to the capital Orugallu. But queen Rudrama fought with him for fifteen days and destroyed the great Seuna cavalry. Mahadeva was chased upto the walls of Devagiri fort by the Kakatiya forces under the command of the queen herself. This victory of Rudrama was borne out by epigraphical evidence as well. A fragmentary inscription in the Bidar fort[64] gives a lengthy description of the Kakatiya kings Rudra, Mahadeva, Ganapatideva who was still alive at that time and his daughter Rudrama a subordinate of the queen nemed Bhairava of the Sinda family is said, in the available portion, to have accompanied Rudrama as a commander of the army in all her expedition. The existence of this epigraph though fragmentary, in the Southern territory of the Seuna kingdom, where no other Kakatiya record has been noticed so far, bears testimony to Rudrama's attack on the Yadava kingdom. Her annexation of the area under the Beda-dakota (Bidar) to the Kakatiya Kingdom indicates that the military enterprise undertaken by her was successful. Unwilling to record the discomfiture of his master, Hemadri glossed it over, by stating that his patron left Rudrama free, because of his reluctance to kill a woman. On the other hand it was the Kakatiya queen who annexed portions of the Yadava kingdom and established her power. Mahadeva sued for peace and agreed to pay Rudrama huge amounts of money and horses as war indemnity. It may further be noted some Yadava chiefs of the royal family like Sarangapanideva, due to their differences with Mahadeva sought asylum in the Andhra country and obtained fiefs by the grace of Rudrama. Recently discovered a grant is Alapadu grant[65] certain Yadava Prince

Ellanadeva who is said to have born in the line Bhillama and Jaitugi was married to a daughter of Kakatiya Rudrama.

After the death of Mahadeva in the last quarter of 1271 A.D., the succession went to his son Amana. But his rule lasted only for a few months. Ramachandra, the son of Kannara or Krishna, overthrew him and forcibly occupied the throne, obviously because he was the rightful heir to it. Possibly because of his young age, Mahadeva assumed power after Kannara's death. But after him, his son Amana claimed the throne and occupied it.

Ramachandra ascended the throne towards the end of 1271 A.D. But his inscription are not unanimous in counting his regnal years.

Ramachandra met with stiffer opposition in his encounters with his eastern rivals, the Kakatiyas. We have seen in the earlier that Mahadeva, far from succeeding in acquiring any territory of the Kakatiyas, suffered a set back. Ramachandra's efforts also in this direction did not meet with success. The Seuna records are silent about the invasion of the Andhra country by Ramachandra; but references to the Seunas in the Kakatiya records and also in Prataparudra Yasobhushana suggest that a fierce battle took place between the two armies and the Seuna armies had a retreat. Besides his hostilities towards that country it appears that Ramachandra even helped the feudatories of the Kakatiya queen who rebelled against her. One such dissident feudatory was the Kayastha chief Ambadeva who, taking advantage of the disturbed conditions of the Kakatiya kingdom, caused by the aggressions of the Pandyas and the Cholas and the rebellious chief within the country tried to became an idependent ruler. It can be gathered from his inscriptions, which mention no overlord, that he fairly succeeded in his endeavour. In one of his records dated 1290 A.D.[66] the feudatories of Rudramba, it is stated that he was adorned by the ornaments of jewels and gold sent by the king of Devagiri. This suggests that Ramachandra encouraged him with considerable financial assistance. But his independent status did not last long. In 1291 A.D. Rudramba force him to submit.[67]

Finally Rudramadevi and her general Mallikarjuna-nayaka killed by Ambadeva who is a Kayasta chief, in a battle by the support of Kakatiya enemies, the Seunas and Pandyas.

Rudramadevi's reign ended with a great rebellion in the kingdom in addition to the disgrace to the royal family.

Prataparudra A.D. 1289-1323. His Contemporary Yadava Rulers were Ramachandra A.D. 1271-1312 Senkaradeva A.D. 1311-1312

The familiar usage Prataparudra was generally called Kumara Rudradeva for several more year even after his assession. He was associated in the military undertakings and the government of his grandmother (Rudramadevi).

After Prataparudra's accession to throne third attack was against the Seuna who supported Ambadeva. The Narasaraopet inscription of Manumagandagopala also credits him with the titles Seuna-Kataka-venu-Kabalana-deva-Pavaka (the wild fire to the bamboo-like army of the Seunas) which obviously hints that he joined the expedition of the Kakatiya monarch against the Seuna kingdom. Some of the important events which took place during this invasion are recorded in an inscription set up in the fort of Raichur by Gonavithala, the Kakatiya feudatory ruling at Vardhamanapura in the Mahbubnagar district. This epigraph is dated Saka 1216 (A.D. 1294) which must be the date of the completion of the construction of the fort. It is clear from this event, which might have taken place some time in 1291 or 1292 A.D., as the construction of fort must have been taken atleast two to three years, that the Seuna army suffered a heavy defeat and the Kakatiyas could encroach upon the Seuna territory. According to this inscription dated S. 1216 (A.D. 1294) Vithala captured the forts of Adavani and Tumbalam in the Bellary district together with Manuva and Haluva in the Raichur doab. After reducing to subjection the chiefs who held sway over this region, Vithala finally entered the city of Raichur, where he is said to have erected a strong fort to protect its inhabitants.[68] It is obvious that Gona Vithala must have wrested the Krishna Tungabhadra doab from the Yadava of Devagiri.

Before Prataparudra consolidate his possession in the South he had to face Muslim invasion from Delhi. Garshap Malik (Ala-ud-din) the son-in-law of Jalal-ud-Din Khalji, the Sultan of Delhi attack on Devagiri, the Yadava capital in A.D. 1295 and seized it. Though he went back to Delhi after exacting heavy sums of money and jewels from king Ramachandra as tribute, he was likely to come again to the South to attack and plunder other Hindu kingdoms. Due to these Muslim incursions there is no more direct conflict between Kakatiyas and Yadava rulers.

Prataparudra succeeded in the Muslim attempt in A.D. 1303. He met the Muslims not less than seven times on the battle field, though he had to make treaties of peace on more than one occasion paying enormous tributes. During the second invasion in 1309 under commander-in-chief or Malik Khafar and Khwaja Haji. Yadava rulers Ramachandra was assisted the Sultans. The seize was began in 19th January A.D. 1310. Prataparudra utterly defeated and made peace with them paid in jewels, horses and elephants agreed to pay tribute. They maintained friendly relations for a long time.

Ramachandra was succeeded by his son Senkaradeva in 1312 A.D. By this time the Seuna kingdom lost its independent status. He had opposed the invader but failed after some time he invited fresh attack from Delhi by withholding the dues to be paid to the Sultan. Malik Khafur invaded and defeated

Senkaradeva inhumanly put to death in 1312 A.D. After the death of Senkaradeva Seuna kingdom annexed to the Muslim empire. Haripaladeva son-in-law of Ramachandra revolted against Sultanate, but Mubarak proceeded in 1318. Mubarak pursued him and captured and brought him before the Sultan and he was put to death.

On the death of Ala-ud-din Khilji Malik Khafur placed the prince Shihab-ud-din on the throne he became as regent but within few days he was murdered, another son of Khilji Shihab-ud-Mubarak Shah seized the throne. He invaded on Telingana in 1318 A.D. becuse Prataparudra stopped to pay tribute due to the frequent changes in Delhi Sultanate. He agreed to pay without any resistance. Mubarak Shah assassinated by Khsraukhan, but Turkish nobles put him to death under Ghiyas-din-Tuglak, the leader of these rebels. He ascended the throne in A.D. 1320. Having consolidate his authority in the kingdom he sent an expedition to Telingana in A.D. 1323 under Ulugh Khan (later Mahammad-bin-Tuglak) to conquere and annex. In the first attempt Ulugh Khan defeated by Prataparudra then Ghiyas-ud-Din Tugluk and Ulugh Khan marched on Telingana, Prataparudra offered stiff fight but defeated. Ulugh-Khan sent Prataparudra to Delhi by his confident officers but before they reach Delhi he died.

With the defeat and death of Prataparudra ended the rule of the Kakatiya line of kings and the country passed into the hands of rulers to belonging to an alien race and religion.

Conclusion

The short sighted policy of these that was largely responsible for the fall of the dynasties race for power and supremacy resulted in unending hostilities amongst contemporary kingdoms. The major powers paramaras, the Gujaras, the Seunas, the Hoyasalas and the Kakatiyas were constantly at war with one another. These fights rather than bringing any advantage resulted in mutual weakening.

Such a hostile attitude towards others was no doubt a traditional and common feature. But atleast the changed circumstances needed a change in outlook and policy especially in view of alien invasions. Absence of organisation and unity led not only to the extinction of the Seunas and Kakatiyas but to the subsequent fall of the Southern kingdoms.

References

1. Annual Report on Epigraphy. 1913-14. C.P. 1 and paras 5 and 6.
2. *Ibid.*, p. 202
3. Inscription of Andhra Pradesh, Warangal district.
4. *Ibid.*, wg. No. 13
5. Epigraphia Indica. IV. p. 91, I, 91.
6. Epigraphia Indica. II. p. 218, verse 10.
7. Rajaprasastri, *op. cit.*, p. 193 verse 22.
8. Epigraphia Indica. Vol. XV. p. 350, Text line 3.
9. Epigraphia Indica. Vol. II. pp. 221ff.
10. Rajaprasastri, *op. cit.*, p. 194, verse 29.
11. Text line B. 5 *(op. cit)*.
12. Eg. El. Vol. XXXII, p. 38.
13. Rajaprasastri, *op. cit.*, p. 194, verse 32.
14. Indian Antiquary, Vol. IX, pp. 12 ff.
15. He vaniquished Dommaraja and captured his town Nagara.
16. Subdued the prowess of Meda and defeated the confederacy of the rival kings.
17. Dr. S.H. Ritti, The Senas of Devagiri.
18. Epigraphia Indica, II. pp. 238 ff.
19. R.G. Bhandarkar. Early History of the Deccan App. c.p. 114.
20. Dr. G. Yazdani Ed. Early History of the Deccan, p. 529 fn.
21. Inscriptions of Andhra Pradesh Karimnagar District.
22. *Ibid.*, wg., 42.
23. Epigraphia Andhrica.
24. Inscriptions of Andhra Pradesh, Karimnagar district.

25. Inscriptions of Andhra Pradesh, Warangal district. 47.
26. Epigraphia Andhrica. IV. p.114, line 36.
27. Epigraphia Indica. III, p. 101.
28. *Ibid.* IV, p. 341 line 5.
29. Indian Antiquary, XIV, p. 316.
30. Epigraphia Indica. III, p. 111.
31. IAP. Kn., 28.
32. EI : XXXII, p. 39 verse 13.
33. Kujat-Shatpada-gita Vaibhava-bharanam Jatastato Jatugi 11, 1, Samaniya Karuna-Varuna—alayab/Priyamvad-asyam—akarot—Kshiten-Ganapati(m) Patim. IA; XIV, p. 314 lines 22-23.
34. P.V.P. Sastry, Kakatiyas of Warangal page 105 lines 3-5.
35. Epigraphia Carnatika; V. B1. 77.
36. EI; III, p. 218.
37. Rice : Mysore inscription : p. 106.
38. EC : VI, Kd. 36.
39. EI. XXV, p. 220.
40. *Ibid* : p. 202.
41. Mysore Archaelogical Survey Report : 1929. p. 142.
42. EC. VIII, Sb. 135, Sewell Historical Inscriptions of South India p. 134., IA., 1892 : pp. 197-98.
43. EI : XIX, p. 23.
44. *Ibid* : XXI, p. 12 : R.G. Bhandarkar EHD (1957) p. 123 : JBBRAS: XII, p. 38.
45. Yazdani, The Early History of the Deccan. p. 612.
46. JAHRS XXIII, p. 91.
47. AR 446 of 1912; AR 1920. Part II para 55.
48. Nirvachanottara Ramayana; 1 verse 33.
49. Dasakumara Charitra I verse 33.
50. EI ; XXX, p. 36.
51. IA; XXI, p. 198.
52. *Ibid.*
53. JAHRS ; XXIII p. 4.
54. EHD; P : os: No. 13 p. 52.
55. Hyderabad Archaeological series; No. 19, Km. 1 and 2.

56. SII ; X No. 370 : AR. 208 of 1905.
57. HAS : No. 4, 4 Verse 22 p. 10.
58. EI.
59. SII; IV, Nos 625 and 627.
60. EHD; p. 612; TT PI No. 53.
61. *Ibid.*
62. AR; 122 of 1826.
63. Dr. N.V. Ramanayya, Perur Inscription, No. 12.
64. P.V.P. Sastry, Select Epigraphy of Andhra Pradesh No. 21.
65. Dr. N. Ramesan, Copper plate Inscriptions of Hyd. Mus. 1 pp. 109 ff.
66. SII., Vol. X, No. 465.
67. Yazdani Ed. EHD.
68. Andhra Pradesh Archaeological Series 3, pp. 101-102.

Bibliography

A Catalogue of Inscriptions (copied upto 1964) by Sri P.V. Parabrahma Sastri.

Andhra Pradesh Government Archaeological Series.

Annual Report of Epigraphy, 1893-1961-62.

Annual Reports of Indian Epigraphy, Delhi, 1945-46 to 1971-72.

Archaeological Series, No. 38 and 39, Hyderabad.

Butterworth, A. and Venugopal Chetty, V. *List of Nellore Inscriptions,* Vol. II, Madras 1905.

Corpus of Telangana Inscriptions, Vol. I to III, Ed. by Dr. P. Srinivasachar, Vol. IV Ed. by M. Somasekhara Sarma.

Epigraphy Andhrica, Vols. I and IV.

Epigraphia Indica, Vols. I, III to IX, XI to XIV, XVI, XVIII to XIX, XXI to XXII, XXV, XXVII to XXVIII, XXXI to XXXII, XXXVI and XXXVIII from 1892-1970, Calcutta.

Gopal, B.R. (Ed.), *Karnataka Inscriptions,* Vol. V.

Hyderabad Archaeological Series, Nos. 6, 8, 16, 19 and 38, Hyderabad (1942 onwards).

Indian Antiquary

Madras Report on Epigraphy 1918-19.

Nellore District Inscriptions.

Parabrahma Sastry, P.V., *Select Epigraphs of Andhra Pradesh* (Archaeological Series No. 31), Hyderabad, 1970.

Parabramha Sastry, "Bidar Inscription of Siddhabhairava" Select Epigraphy of Andhra Pradesh.

Rama Rao, M., *Inscription of Andhradesa,* Vol. II, Part I.

Ramesan, N. (Ed.), *Copper Plate Inscriptions of the Andhra Pradesh State Museum,* Vols. I and II, Hyderabad 1962 and 1970.

Ramesan, N., "Studies in Medieval Deccan History" based on two new unpublished copper plate inscriptions of the State Museum, Vol. III, Government of Andhra Pradesh, 1972 (Archaeological Series No. 29).

Rangacharya, V., (Ed.) *A topographical List of the Inscriptions of the Madras Presidency,* Vols. I, II and III, Madras, 1919 (The Inscriptions of this list is referred to as No. 10 of V.R.).

Rice, B.L. (Ed.), *Epigraphia Carnatica,* Vols. II, IV and VII, Bangalore.

Sircar, D.C. (Ed.), *Select Inscriptions.*

South Indian Inscriptions, Vol. IV, V, VIX and XII.

South Indian Inscriptions, Vol. I, III to XII, XIX to XX and XXIII (from 1890 onwards), Madras.

Telangana Inscriptions Ed. by Lakshmanaraya Parisodaka Mandali, Hyderabad.

Venkata Ramanayya, N., Peruru Inscriptions, Nos. 3, 7 and 15.

Venkataramanayya, N., *Andhra Pradesh Government Report on Epigraphy for* 1965., (Epigraphy Series No. 1), Hyderabad, 1968.

Primary Sources—Literary

Ekamaranatha *Prataparudracharitramu*

Jayapa Senani *Nrtta Ratnavali*

Kolani Ganapatideva	*Svagoyasaramu*
Palkuriki Somanatha	*Basavapuranamu*
Palkuriki Somanatha	*Panditaradhya charitramu*
Srinatha	*Palnativiracharitra*

Secondary Sources: Published Works

Appadorai, A., *Economic Conditions in South India,* Vol. I, Madras, 1936.

Bhandarkar, R.G., *The Early History of the Dekkan,* 3rd edition, Calcutta, (1924).

Dikshitar, V.R.R., *Hindu Administrative Institutions,* Madras, 1929.

Dikshit, G.S., *Local Self Government in Medieval,* Karnataka, Dharwad, 1964.

Gopalakrishna, S., *The Sculpture of the Kakatiyas,* Hyderabad, 1964.

Karashima Noboru (Ed.), *Indus Valley to Mekiong Delta: Explorations in Epigraphy,* Madras, 1985.

Kerashima, N., South Indian History and Society: Studies from Inscriptions A.D. 850-1800, Oxford University Press, Delhi, 1984.

Kuppuswamy, G.R., Economic conditions in Karnataka (A.D. 973-1336), Karnatak University, Dharwar, 1975.

Mahalingam, T.V., *South Indian Polity* (Madras, 1956).

Majumdar, A.K., Chalukyas of Gujarat (A Survey of the History and Culture of Gujarat from the middle of the 10th to the end of the 13th Century), Bombay, 1956.

Narasimha Murty, A.V., *Seunas of Devagiri* (Mysore, 1971).

Nilakanta Sastri, K.A., *A History of South India,* 3rd edition (Madras, 1966).

Nilakanta Sastri, K.A., *Colas,* 2nd edition (Madras, 1953).

Nilakanta Sastri, K.A., *Development of Religion in South India* (Calcutta, 1963).

Nilakanta Sastri, K.A., *A History of South India from Prehistoric Times to the Fall of Vijayanagar,* Madras, 1955.

Parabrahma Sastry, P.V., *The Kakitiyas of Warangal* (Hyderabad, 1978).

Ramachandra Rao, C.V., *Administration and Society in Medieval Andhra A.D. 1038-1538* under *The Eastern Gangas and The Surya Vamsa Gajapatis,* Nellore, 1976.

Ramesh, K.V., *A History of South Ķarnataka,* Dharwar, 1970.

Shanmụgam, P., Aspects of the Chola Revenue System in Karnataka, Eds. A.V. Narasimha Murthy, K.V. Ramesh, Giridharasri, Agam Kala Prakashan, Delhi, 1987, pp. 123-128.

Sircar, D.C., *Indian Epigraphical Glossary,* Delhi, 1966.

Vaidehi Krishna Murty, A., *Social and Economic Conditions in Eastern Deccan (A.D. 1000-1250),* Secunerabad, 1970.

Venkateswara Rao, T., *Local Bodies in Medieval Andhra, from A.D. 1000-1336,* Hyderabad 1987.

Venkateswara, S.V., *Indian Culture Through the Ages,* Vol. I, London, 1928.

Partibha, M., *Unpublished Doctoral Thesis,* Rudramadevi (Submitted to the Andhra University, Waltair, 1971).

Journals and Proceedings

Bharati

Indian Economic and Social History Review

Itihas

Journal of Ancient Indian History and Culture

Journal of Andhra Historical Research Society
Journal of Andhra History and Culture
Journal of Indian Antiquary, Bombay
Journal of Indian Historicla Quarterly
Journal of Indian History
Journal of the Epigraphical Society of India
Proceedings of Indian History Congress
Studies in History
Subhashi
The Indian Historical Quarterly

Index